PRINTHOUSE BOOKS
PRESENTS:

JUMPOFF

I0161322

Jara Everett

2nd Edition

VIP INK Publishing Group, Inc.

Atlanta, GA.

Jara Everett

WWW.PRINTHOUSEBOOKS.COM

Hip Hop's Mistress

Tells all....

VIP INK PUBLISHING GROUP, INC.

PRINTED IN THE USA.

JUMPOFF

NON-FICTION

Cover art designed by SK7.

Published 4-28-13

Library of Congress Cataloging-in-Publication data.

Jara Everett   Jumpoff; Hip Hop's Mistress; Tells all!

1.Urban Literature 2.African American

3.Auto Biography 4.Women 5.Erotica

PRINTHOUSE BOOKS, ATLANTA,GA.

Jara Everett; Hip Hop's Mistress releases her first Tell all Auto Biography; taking you on a journey into the world of Hip Hop and Entertainment from Chicago, Miami, LA to Atlanta. You will experience laughter, disbelief and erotic pleasures as she shares her experiences with R. Kelly, Suge Knight, Tupac, Martin Lawrence, Young Jeezy, Shawty Redd, Jazze Pha, Too Short, Gary Busey and more in this epic tell all; adequately titled Jumpoff!

THE REAL (TRUTH)

My life with, R. KELLY, MARTIN LAWRENCE,
YOUNG JEEZY, SUGE KNIGHT, TUPAC,
SHAWTY REDD, JAZZE PHA
AND OTHERS

VOLUME 1

JUMPOFF

JARA EVERETT

2ND EDITION

JUMPOFF

DEDICATION

I thank God, for the wisdom, strength and blessings he has graced me with. Each person in this book gave life to who I was and who I am. I have had the opportunity to live, understand life, see the world, to learn, and to grow from these experiences which have inspired me to write this book and help others learn to see themselves and be better than who they are now.

JUMPOFF

CONTENTS

ACKNOWLEDGMENTS

Simeon Rogers, Laketha Everett, Robin West, Kimi Rhochelle, Lori Cole and Donald Neville, thanks for your help every step of the way in making all of this possible. To my family, I will always love you forever. To all who have supported me, thank you so much!! Your support has truly been good to me.

Finally, I want to thank Brian Sandy. Thanks a million, Brian, for your expertise, guidance, and support at a time when I really needed an editor, and for your patience in putting up with my concerns about my project, and my queries about this and that, and for twisting my words, and on and on. It's been a real pleasure. (Yeah, but get ready for Volume 2.)

See Brian Sandy's blog--**blackamericanfiction.wordpress.com**--or email him at <u>urbanbookdoctor@yahoo.com</u> for help with your novel or writing project.

Jara Everett

1

AFFECTED BY CHILDHOOD

Growing up I had a mother who was very strict and very protective of me, which caused me to rebel and over react to situations. I must say that when I was fifteen I gave her a run for her money. I was young, dumb, and had a crush on a young man named Bruce, who was nineteen at the time. My mother knew I was hot and easily influenced, so she kept a tight leash on me, to keep me away from falling into teenage pregnancy.

Because she was so strict with me, at every given opportunity, I would sneak out of the house at nighttime and not return until early morning hours. I lived in a three-story house and the basement was a way to escape through the windows. I would wait until my parents fell asleep to sneak outside late nights. I suppose I had done it one too many times, because the neighbor three houses down drove by one night and saw me sneaking out of the window.

One night my parents had fallen to sleep around ten o'clock. Sure, I crawled through the window and walked four blocks to Bruce's house. He lived with his mother, and clearly, I can remember her not caring who he would bring into the house. He would walk me straight in, past her, and into his bedroom.

At fifteen, I knew nothing about sex. I was only having sex because this guy wanted it. In fact, I was a long way from learning what an orgasm would feel like. It was all about Bruce, not me. The only time we spent together was when we had sex. I didn't mind because, as long as I was around him, it didn't matter what he wanted.

After we had sex one night, he only walked me to the corner where I lived at because he didn't want my parents to see him. I walked home the rest of the way. By the time I made it to the house and saw the basement lights on, I knew I was in big trouble.

So, instead of walking to the house, I took a detour and walked over to the next block. I heard music coming from a house near where I was walking, so I stopped and decided to put my acting role on. Two guys came on the front porch, and I fell out on the sidewalk. I could hear the two guys walking over to me because I was clearly aware of what I was doing.

I heard one guy ask the other guy if I was breathing. Then the two guys picked me up by the feet and the back and carried me up to their house. I heard one guy saying, "Momma, Momma, we found this girl laying out on the sidewalk."

I was still pretending to be unconscious, but I could hear everything going on. The mother of the man who found my crazy behind laid out onto the pavement of the sidewalk called the police and the ambulance. It only took the ambulance a few minutes to arrive.

I'd carried an identification card on me, so I remember the ambulance announcing my name to someone while on their radio. I was carried out on a stretcher into the ambulance truck.

As soon as we arrived at the hospital, the doctor treated me immediately. I was in the ER for at least two hours. I believe I had even fallen asleep at one point. If this was a role in a major film, I would have won an Oscar for best actress because, no matter what, not even the doctor could wake me up with the smelling salts.

Moments later, I heard the doctor in the hallway talking to a voice that sounded like my mother's. My eyes were still shut at this point. Soon the voice got closer up on me. I heard the doctor say, "Mother, I even used smelling salts to awake her, and she still did not wake up. We tried everything we could to bring her to and she will not wake up." The doctor had even said that my vital signs were all normal and they didn't know what else to do.

Then my mother got right up in my face and said, "I know what to do." That scared me so bad, I woke up. I mean, I was literally scared of my mother because she didn't play that sympathy role. The doctor told my mother that this was truly amazing because he'd tried everything to wake me up and it didn't work. I remember being grounded for a very long time for pulling that stunt.

Another time I was caught out late at night was when my parents went out. Usually, if they went out, they would stay for a while. Well, not this particular night. They made it home before me, so I had to pull another stunt to get out of punishment.

This particular night, I walked all the way to the police station and pretended to be crazy. I told the police I couldn't go home because there was a big black thing in the doorway of the house, that he would get me if I tried to go inside the house. The police asked me where I lived and also wanted my parents' phone number. I told him I could not remember the house phone number, but I could remember my home address. So the police took me to the house and parked across the street from the house.

When the officer opened the back of the squad car for me to get out, I screamed out to him and pretended that the big black thing was standing in the doorway on the front porch, but there was nothing there. The officer then went up to the house and rang the doorbell. My mother answered the door. I tried to hide, sitting in the backseat of the squad car.

The officer told my mother I was afraid to get out of the car because of the big black thing at the house. Well, because my mother knew me, she told the officer there was nothing wrong with me, that I was trying to make a fool of him and everyone else. The officer told her that I was really scared and really felt that something was wrong because I was screaming out of the car that a big black thing was at the house.

I guess my mother got tired of hearing that load of mess. She told the officer that I was right, that there was a big black thing at the house and that the big black thing happened to be her. So the police would not release me to my parents because I was crying like never before.

My mother told him that they need to take me back to the station because if she had gotten a hold of me that night she would halfway beat me down. The officer took me back to the police station and released me to a social worker. The social worker called my parents and asked if there was a relative's house where I could stay until my mother calmed down from being angry with me. My mother gave them my aunt's number, and my aunt picked me up from the police station, and I stayed at her place all night.

Basically, I was hardheaded in many ways, tried to fool my parents because I felt my mother was a little too strict on me. But I am glad she was.

2

A RELATIONSHIP BUILT ON LIES

Once upon a time, I got through a two-year relationship unsuccessfully. Yes, I had a JUMPOFF who didn't mind me knocking him off here and there while I was involved in a relationship. I didn't want to be with the JUMPOFF I was dealing with because he wouldn't last long enough for me to have sexual intercourse after giving me oral. I was involved in a relationship with a guy I cared for. He worked in the music industry as a sound engineer and worked with some known rappers and singers in the industry.

A little over two years in the relationship, this

guy wanted me to watch porno with him and I did. He always had this fantasy of me being with another guy while he watched. But his fantasy was to have me blow a guy with a big dome. I am a pleaser so that would be a piece of cake for me. After several weeks passed, he wanted to have sex while watching porno a lot. I didn't have a problem with it in the beginning, but after a while it was taking over my sexual pique for him.

He could never get me off, so each time we had sex, I had to get myself off with a "pocket rocket." I never did see the concept of him wanting me to suck on another man in front of him. I needed to understand where he was coming from, so I would talk sex-talk about other men's penises to him. One night he wanted me to watch porno with him again and I did. So I got a gut feeling that this was pretty weird. Guys usually want another female in the bedroom, not another man. I decided to do the ultimate test. When he would turn on the porno and ask me if I wanted to feel another man's dome in my mouth, I said yes, as long as he would do it with me. I asked him if he would suck on

10

another man's dome with me, and he said if I wanted him to, he would do it.

Okay, that threw me but I had to keep it cool. I know how much he wanted to please me, and I wanted him to mean what he said instead of agreeing to something he thought I would like for him to do.

A few months passed and he asked me if I had any male friends I could do it with while he watched. Well, I did have several friends who would have loved for me to blow them, but of course I said no. I thought he was out to test me, test the things I would do. I encouraged him to find someone, maybe one of his friends.

One day he called me up because a friend of his sent over a picture of his penis. He forwarded me the text and asked me if it was big enough for me to suck on. I pretended it was big enough for me.

The next week came, and he forwarded me a

video of his friend ejaculating. Again, I thought to myself, *What man does that?* It all seemed odd to me. Still going along with his little fetish, I told him I would suck his friend's dome, as long as he would do it with me, and again he said yes.

By this time we had talked about getting married and everything. I even went along with obtaining a marriage license. It just did not feel right to see, or to know I had a guy who I was going to marry be with another man.

Later, after we obtained a marriage license, he called me up and said he had met a guy who was into the same thing we were into. Now, mind you, we had never done the swingers thing. So I played along with the little story he told me.

He asked me, could he go over to meet the guy at his place just to talk and see what he was on. I asked to go with him, but he said he felt more comfortable going alone. My voice must have given a signal of me not liking that he would even consider such a thing with another man. I tried to convince him that it would make me feel better to go along with him, but he didn't feel comfortable with that.

My ex did say to me that if I did not want him to go over to the swingers' house that he would not do it. But I insisted that he go there anyways, because I knew he would find a way to do it regardless.

So I led him to believe that everything was good with me knowing he wanted to go over and test this guy out without me. All the while I had a huge problem with it and did not understand what was it inside of him that made him want to suck on another man's penis. It was disgusting for me to think about it, because I thought he was a straight man. How could I tell someone, this guy likes penis, that's what I was thinking. Little did he know, I was planning on leaving him eventually. My mind was already made up.

So as he was leaving, I asked him to take some pictures and send it to me. He never did take pictures, but he did video tape it. Sure enough, he called me over to his place. I took my time getting there. I was trying to figure out how I was going to handle the situation. When I finally made it there, he had just gotten out of the shower still with a towel wrapped around his body.

We sat on the bed, and I asked him to let me see the video tape. Sure enough he had taped five segments of him and the other guy going at it. When I saw the guy I thought was a heterosexual for over two years bobbing his head on another's man's penis I was like, *OMG! Really dude! So, this is what you like? Vaginas and penises?*

I had to ask him, when did he realize he was bisexual, because that is something you should tell someone up front and let them decide if they want to deal with it or not. He said since he had been with me, because he had never been with anyone as sexy as me. What a bucket of crap to tell anyone!

I asked him if it was good, and he said it was

okay. But he definitely can't see himself sucking a man's penis every day. By the looks of the video tape, he looked like an amateur bobbing his head on the man's penis, but the other guy in the video was a pro. I also knew he was lying about how good it felt because his penis was rock-hard on the video tape. As I told him, I have no problems with gays or a bisexual, but how can I compete with a man wanting to suck on another man's penis?

He was so weak, I knew he would blame me if I left him. He would say that I tricked him into sucking another man's penis. He would have also said that he only did it because he thought that's what I wanted. Come on, if I had told him to jump off a cliff, knowing he would die, would he have done it? Excuses.

So from then on for the next week I started to avoid him a lot. Still we had planned on getting married, and it was just two weeks away before we were to wed. Every time I saw him, all I thought about was, *My dude is gay. Damn!* It confused me so bad, I was even with him after I knew he was sucking on another man's penis.

Then I thought about it and asked him if he would try to have sex with another man. He said he didn't know but maybe he could try it. That really sealed it then. I knew I had to end it. Because, at that point, he was like a bitch even more. That relationship was a straight-up mess. I stopped calling him altogether, and he called me a hundred times and I never answered his calls.

Finally, he contacted my sister and pretended like I was the worst person on the planet. Although my sister didn't know what transpired between us, my cousin did. All the time he dogged my character out to her, he never told the real truth, which was, he liked to get down with men.

Sure, I wasn't perfect. I had a little JUMPOFF in between our relationship, but that was too much for me to handle. I don't have a penis, so the whole relationship was built on a lie. Every relationship I was ever in was built on me or the other person having a JUMPOFF. That's just the way it's been for me.

In hindsight, there were always signs such as when we would go to the store and I would catch my ex eyeing another man. I thought it was strange but never paid too much attention to it because I had never been with a bisexual man, as far as I know.

There was another time where my ex was at the gym and he told me it was because I was so sexy when he sees another man with a nice penis he thinks about me being with him.

3

BEEN THERE, DONE THAT

Just when we thought we had seen it all, now there is this— JUMPOFFS. I have heard many people ask this question: What is a JUMPOFF?

Well, for starters, I could give you my version of a JUMPOFF, which is a person who doesn't give a damn about what anybody thinks about them while they're getting whatever it is they need.

Urban Dictionary defines a JUMPOFF as any

human body having sexual contact/encounter with another human body other than their significant other. In simple terms, someone you cheat with, like a mistress, or someone you might have on the side.

In most cases, the term JUMPOFF is associated with being a woman, but could also be a man. Alternatively, some of you might have your own version of a JUMPOFF, which I will get to later in the book.

People usually use the word JUMPOFF in a derogatory way. Most of us have heard that a JUMPOFF is known to be the downfall of plenty of relationships—in politics, professional sports, in the entertainment industry, and in the corporate world. Well, hold on a second, isn't that how a lot of people in America operate?

I would think that Americans have the highest rates of divorce due to their lack of communication skills, and infidelity. Husbands and wives are afraid to tell each other when something is lacking or going left in their relationship, that could draw either of them to seek the attention of a JUMPOFF.

In many opinions, JUMPOFFS are self-seeking, only thinking of themselves. Hmmm. Again, we are talking about the world here, people.

Now with all of that said about a JUMPOFF, why would anyone choose to be one? I have the best, simplest, most philosophical answer to that question. One might choose to be a JUMPOFF to get ahead in life. While you are in the process of doing so, you simply should not give a rat's ass what people say about you. Then again, you have those who prefer not to be in a relationship, but they will see a few people for certain needs. Some people do not want to be in a committed relationship but would see someone from time to time. If they aren't in a committed relationship, they won't have the problems of dealing with demands or questions like the five W's phrase.

There are many reasons why a person would be a

JUMPOFF or have a JUMPOFF. Most of our successful careers lead us into the realm of temptation by many beautiful women and men. I do know that the greater a man's opportunity, the more he might cheat. So when you have a man with a whole lot of money and power, you will see JUMPOFFS coming out of the woodwork like ambulance chasers. That is why the producers, actors, ballplayers, directors, executives, etc… who see a pretty face with a banging body will get at you, even though they have the perfect "pretend life" at home, with the perfect wife and kids—the truth about your man, he is not the perfect mate you want to believe he is.

So don't hate on the JUMPOFF, ladies! These men just want to have it all.

Now to those who choose to be a JUMPOFF, yes, it can sometimes get you a quick come-up to where the spotlight will shine on you. Typically, your 15 minutes of fame has arrived, so milk the cow for what it's worth, baby.

Just take a broad look at certain individuals who

have climbed their way up from nothing because they were a JUMPOFF at some point. Hello!

But keep in mind that what works for some JUMPOFFS might not always work for others as they try to get ahead. I will say, if you decide to be a JUMPOFF, be the best at what you do, boo. It's your life, and at the end of the day, you will have to live with the choices you have made.

You have some people who fall into the category of being an unintentional JUMPOFF because some guys are slick enough to keep their main chick a secret. When you do find out the truth, it is hard to halt from the situation because by then your heart is involved. That's how you will become the unintentional JUMPOFF.

You have to love America. It tickles me because America has proven to the world that JUMPOFFS exist no matter where you're at. All the way from that big old ugly White House in D.C., to the hood streets in every city, somewhere there is a JUMPOFF.

Not too long ago, one of our former presidents was in a lot of heat because he chose to deal with a JUMPOFF named Monica. I am sure we all remember that scandal and the big media frenzy surrounding it.

This is no secret to the world. I shake my head because we forget so easily as time goes by. Luckily for the former president, his JUMPOFF relationship had no damaging effect on his personal life, as far as we know. By the same token, he lost the respect of many who had helped him gain the highest and most powerful office in America, if not the world.

What was the intention of his JUMPOFF? Not money, nor did it appear to be for power. Only Monica would know the reason as to why she was out to be the former president's JUMPOFF. I do not have the facts to say what her intentions were, but if I had to guess, I would say she was just hot for him and wanted her moment to have with a man in a powerful position. I mean, I have to say Bill was good-looking back then, and had a little soul.

In return, this JUMPOFF named Monica did know how to play her deck of cards. She held on tight to the ace of spades until it was time to lay it out on the table. Somewhere in the mix, she felt the need to pull the ace of spades out—the former president's DNA stain on her dress.

Some cow feeder—I am referring to one of Monica's so-called friends—somehow convinced her to kiss and tell on the former president. In exchange, she would get her 15 minutes of fame. Well, this is America. The country of liberty that tells you to be all you can be. Seems to me we've upheld that speech and put it to good use.

So now we know that the political world also has its JUMPOFFS too. They primarily have scandals to break out around election time. Before we get to my life, I feel the need to touch on these areas to remind you that JUMPOFFS are not in the entertainment industry alone—they are everywhere, and in all walks of life.

I have observed the differences between a celebrity JUMPOFF, an everyday next door neighbor JUMPOFF, and a hood JUMPOFF. We quickly tend to excuse the mess celebrity JUMPOFFS create because they are on TV.

Some celebrity JUMPOFFS wreck their families, but guess what? We continue to support them and buy their products. It doesn't prevent actors from earning a living either, because we would still pay to see them on screen just because of who they are, and we will love them regardless of what they do.

Now let the JUMPOFF in the neighborhood do the same thing. We do not treat them the same as we would treat a celebrity JUMPOFF.

We think that a neighborhood JUMPOFF is the most scandalous somebody we know, although this neighborhood JUMPOFF has done no more dirt than the celebrity JUMPOFF. It is unfair, but as we know, JUMPOFFS are often judged by the different classes they fall in. Some people feel that if you are rich and powerful, you could have a pass for being a JUMPOFF.

Here are the levels of classes a JUMPOFF would fall into. The entertainment industry JUMPOFFS are in the Class A. When the Class A JUMPOFFS becomes romantically involved with a famous actor or a person in music, it creates a media frenzy for months. (I understand it can be tough on male celebrities when the groupies come after them.)

Everyone wants to know which celebrity is out there being naughty, and who that celebrity has let into his or her world of entertainment. They also want to know how JUMPOFFS get so close to that inner circle. You might talk about that JUMPOFF at the time and use every inferior name you can find, but I believe that half of America would date a superstar if the opportunity arose, even if they had someone else at home.

I am not saying that you would go as far as to have sex with the entertainer, but given the opportunity to be close to the subject, who would not jump at it? Just know that if you would go outside the cubicle area and give up your jewel, you are certainly classified as a JUMPOFF, whether you want to see it that way or not.

JUMPOFFS in the political world are in Class B because politicians have less media attention on their infidelities than those in the entertainment industry. Most of us could care less if Governor "whoever" is dating "whatever."

The Class B JUMPOFFS often holds an ace of spades, somewhat like Monica. They will hold on to their card until that politician is ready to pursue office. Then pull it out of the woodwork to destroy that person from moving ahead. This occurs when a JUMPOFF wants their 15 minutes of fame, or because that person didn't do enough to please the JUMPOFF.

For the life of me, I cannot understand how a political figure can have a wife and kids they claim to love so dearly and still have a JUMPOFF. Then they cry like a baby when they get caught in the action, even though they already knew what the fallout would be like. I suggest they own up to what they're doing.

So to all of you politicians who know you have to get your vote from the people, and you got your little JUMPOFF on the side, thinking you got the best of both worlds, think again. Because if you do not handle your JUMPOFF as he/she sees fit, somewhere down the line, something will go sour between you and your JUMPOFF.

Knowing you have more to lose than your JUMPOFF does, why be foolish enough to say "screw it" to them? When you do that, you are saying *adiós* to your career, and you stand a strong chance of losing your family. What sense does that make? If you love your family so dearly, and you love the people so much, do not fool around with a JUMPOFF. You will not win. Keep your slim jim in your jockey.

Class C JUMPOFFS live to be the cackling ducks for professional athletes, the biggest players out there. Even the so-called pimps have nothing on them. Professional athletes are too easy to figure out. They go from city to city, field to field, and JUMPOFF to JUMPOFF. Literally. So it's more difficult for the media to cover those scandals than cover an entertainer's JUMPOFF story.

Then too, professional sports players will not lose a position for fooling around with a JUMPOFF, like a politician would. It is part of the game. It is a sad feeling for the players' wives who are oblivious and blinded by their deceitful husbands, especially for those who pretend they don't know what their player husband is all about. You better believe, puss hooks are dragging them in.

The best thing for the player's wives to do is uphold the vow "for better or worse" and live by it.

Just think of it like this, wives—"for better" is the big house, nice cars, lavish bank account, foreign travel, and popping out babies for your down-the-line financial stability after your player husband has left you.

"For worse" is when you pay expensive plastic surgeon bills for repairing bags underneath your eyes for crying your heart out, fixing up your body from having babies so you can still appeal to your player husband, and arguing a lot with him because he won't stop seeing his JUMPOFF.

Always remember, you will not change a player until he is ready to change. JUMPOFFS do lurk after the ballplayers, so the temptation is ever present.

I got news for the ballplayers. If you got JUMPOFFS, enjoy the moment because, once you no longer have a career in professional sports, the JUMPOFF leaves. You are now a no-name person, so the JUMPOFF is off to the next dupe. So I would say to the players with wives, straighten your act up, and get smart. When it's all over with, you will need your wife or somebody who truly loves you to be there for you.

The Class D JUMPOFFS would be the regular everyday neighborhood type, whose story is only important to them and not to the rest of the world. The media don't report on little ol' folks who get involve with JUMPOFFS because they will not make any money to cover such a story.

They would have to mention a non-important Joe Blow, who no one knows, every minute of the hour. Who has the time for that, when they can instantly cover a superstar's irrational lifestyle? The media can be cold and unfair, but as I see it, so is life.

As for me, I think the most beautiful thing of all is learning how to forgive. I say that with a big smile. Just look at what is happening today. We might know some rappers who are in a relationship and see them with their JUMPOFF. In the beginning, we think the worst of that JUMPOFF, but later we start loving the damn JUMPOFF. Then that same JUMPOFF becomes a celebrity for demolishing someone else's so-called happy home because people have talked about this muddy relationship so much, it made the JUMPOFF famous. I am smiling again, because only in America, people will make you a star for being grimy.

Some people live by the name JUMPOFF and feed off having such a name, even though others view them as a muddy hound dog that sniffs after a big superstar. And then they themselves often turn into celebrities we love to follow.

Call it what you want, baby doll. Still, I say if the shoe fits, wear it. I call this a come-up. I will never hate on a JUMPOFF who is out to get what they need. I have done it, and will do it again if I feel I need to. Now there is food for the haters, and you better duck if you don't want more of this to hit you.

4

THE TRUTH BEHIND THE LIES

By no means am I here to say that what a person does is right or wrong, because it's their decision to make. I am just introducing you to the world of JUMPOFFS.

For the men, maybe this book could give you a change in attitude when it comes to infamous JUMPOFFS who will wreck your families. If you don't want that to happen, stop demanding sex from them.

You already know that most people who want a career in the entertainment industry are hungry and thirsty. Many people cannot afford to pay their way through the door with cash money, so if you're asking for sex, you will most likely get it.

So what will a hungry and thirsty young female do to have that success in the entertainment industry? Of course, use her moneymaker. Screwing a person who can help you is better than screwing a different so-called boyfriend all the time that you have to feed with your McDonald's paycheck. I'm not talking bird language here.

If someone calls you a whore because you are after something greater than a fast-food paycheck that you can barely feed a family of two on, oh well, let them preach. If you're screwing anyway, you might as well screw somebody who is willing to help you.

Some of you might say, "Well, she is not trying to send a positive message here at all." And my response is, neither the big mega movie writers or producers try to send the viewers a positive message. But viewers still run to the theaters to watch their movies.

But whoever said in order to write a book, you must send a positive message. This book is not about sending a positive message, but if it does, wonderful. This book is about JUMPOFFS, my life, how I have been a JUMPOFF, and how I have had JUMPOFFS.

I felt like letting you in on knowing how I grappled with in the entertainment industry, rather it is positive or negative, it happened, and that is why I know so much about JUMPOFFS and a whole lot of other things.

Now, seeing that I have gone through so many experiences, I would hope that some of you in these situations and those of you who want to have a role, in the entertainment industry realize what it takes.

We know that JUMPOFF stands for all of the

names mentioned and other disparaging names not mentioned. No matter how you look at it, a JUMPOFF is a JUMPOFF, just like a thief is a thief, and a liar is a liar.

Now a little off course here, but a statement was made that JUMPOFFS share a common trait with vampires. This came from a renowned theology professor I know. Which University did the professor friend attend, he has yet to mention. But the way we fell into this discussion is because I was relating to him my experiences in life as an entertainer.

At first, I thought maybe I had too much wine to drink that day. I did ask the professor to please explain his theory. He explained, by saying "by the sound of it, vampires and JUMPOFFS have both been around for centuries."

Now I don't believe in vampires, and I don't know of any JUMPOFFS who suck blood from another human to cure their starvation. Neither have I as a JUMPOFF.

I have known of JUMPOFFS and a whole lot of

other people sucking on something else for their own indulgence and desire, if you know what I mean. So to the renowned professor who compared vampires to JUMPOFFS, you need to lay low, buddy, and lay off the caffeine. Since I am writing about the story of my life, I had to address that theory the professor threw out to me.

I thought it was necessary to write this book to inform you of what to expect when involved in the entertainment industry.

I do know that sometimes we fall short and end up in a path of darkness. If you stay on a path of darkness, we all know that could lead to destruction. I started that path, walked it, and then got off of it. Got back on it again, then jumped off again.

The way you fall into a dark path such as a JUMPOFF, is mainly due to the fact that you do not know when a lying bastard is lying. Point blank. As I said before, it has happened to me too, although if I had to be a JUMPOFF, it was no sweat for me to be one. But I also fell into a pack of lies as well from a guy who hid the fact that he had a chick already at home.

For most people, by the time they realize that they are the victim in this situation, they are an unpremeditated JUMPOFF. By then, it is hard to break away from that situation because now their heart is into it. Sometimes a guy will burn your ears up with lies just to have you hang around for his pleasure.

Many people have been stuck in this kind of situation all because of lies and deception. It is a terrible feeling to be involved with someone who pretends they are single when truthfully, the person is already involved in a relationship with someone else other than you. Now knowing this person has lied to you, and you do know the truth, how would you resolve this situation? Because you know once a person lies once, more lies have to follow behind that lie.

Usually the other lies follow up like this. "Oh,

I'm in the middle of a divorce," or "I don't plan on being with that person. I just need to get some things together first before I bounce," or "Me and that person sleep in separate rooms until the builder is done building my other house." Please, spare me the drama.

Before you know it, you will have exhausted 2 years with the same jackass singing the same old tune. Only a fool would continue to fall for that muddled crap.

So after hearing all the fabrications this person is telling you, do you sit around and cry all day, every day from being miffed, or do you stay with this person hoping that he or she will leave the main piece after a while to be with you?

You already know that if you stay with the situation, you are the side piece and that makes you one of the JUMPOFFS, whom is in a state of denial that you are an unintentional JUMPOFF.

Again, there are a lot of situations out here like

this, and a lot of people will stay with the jackass. You would actually hear them say, "There is no way I could be the JUMPOFF because I did not know he had someone else in the picture." Oh, please. I am still smiling.

So because the jackass has lied about his situation, you are now compelling yourself to stay in the relationship with him. Well, you have just subjected yourself to be that man's unintentional JUMPOFF. Then, to top it all off, you think that giving the liar an ultimatum to choose between you and his main chick, who you had no idea existed, will make a difference. In all truth, it will not change who and what you are.

Okay, let me soften up a little bit here for the more sensitive people. I know, when a person has been lied to, and they want to give an ultimatum, it is usually because they want to buy more time to prepare themselves for grief. This is how most ultimatums come into play by the enforcer, referring to the JUMPOFF who finds out they've been lied to. "It's either me or the other chick." Well, I will say, since the other chick had this man first, let her keep that perpetual liar.

However, even after giving an ultimatum to the perpetual liar to leave his number one chick, he has at home to be with you, how can you be so sure that he won't do the same thing to you that he has done to his main chick? And if he doesn't break it off with his main chick to be with you, what would you do? Would you still hang in there to dry up like a prune? But to let you tell it, you could never be anybody's JUMPOFF. You might want to rethink that one real long and hard.

I get a thrill out of making it known to that person that they are no better than the JUMPOFF who goes and seeks someone who is already wedged. And that JUMPOFF is the same one that you and your girlfriend have sat around and talked about, and now you are wearing that JUMPOFFS shoes.

So with that said, it does not matter what you think you know about yourself, or what excuses you like to make for staying in a relationship, knowing you are a piece of ass on the side. At this point, you've graduated from an unintentional JUMPOFF to a stamped, state-sealed, certified, in-denial JUMPOFF. Now I am laughing, and I love it.

Being a JUMPOFF at this point is not something you dreamt of being, but it is what it is. Although you might not have known it going into this situation, you know how to rear up and hike away once you find out you are the second lingering piece in this wedged perfidy. No one is stopping you from leaving the situation.

On the other hand, some JUMPOFFS do seek to take your significant other away from your so-called happy home. I say so-called happy home because if it were a happy home, neither he nor she would have a JUMPOFF in the first place. How successful would a JUMPOFF be at captivating your significant other? That depends on how durable your relationship is.

Or imagine you leave your significant other for the JUMPOFF, and then you believe you got something good, right. Well, you are in for a big surprise because that same JUMPOFF is on the way to the next victim. So, to all you players, know what you are working with when you are messing around with a professional JUMPOFF like me when I want to be, before you classify yourself as Big Willie.

Predictably, your relationship with a premeditated JUMPOFF will not work. You will always have it in the back of your mind how you propertied the JUMPOFF. You will be sucked dry and left alone if you do not have, or cannot provide, everything a JUMPOFF needs. I know.

I will just flat out tell you, player—Don't ever leave your girl for a professional JUMPOFF. Once you are sucked dry of all your goods, that JUMPOFF is on to the next. Professional JUMPOFFS can switch on and off like that, like a remote control changing a TV channel.

Now that you know the meaning of a JUMPOFF, and we know the different types of

JUMPOFFS, let's modify JUMPOFFS to know what their jobs consist of.

The main job of a JUMPOFF is to "customize" a person to satisfy their own desires. Typically, a JUMPOFF will jump on your ship and have you collapse before you hit shore. But that's not true for all JUMPOFFS.

Again, I am in no way saying how you should live your life. This book is for those of you who already know what a JUMPOFF is and for those of you who do not know. For those of you petrified of knowing that JUMPOFFS do exist, you might really need to tune in to this book.

JUMPOFFS are the reason why a lot of women have so many infidelity problems with their loved ones. If I had a loved one, I would simply ask him if he has a JUMPOFF. I'm not a jealous person at all, so if a dude I was seeing had a JUMPOFF, so be it. Have it your way. At least I know.

What I have realized is that a lot of people are afraid to have any type of discussion about

JUMPOFFS. But it is no secret to our society, and shouldn't be treated as such.

Anybody can be a JUMPOFF, like an actor or actress, a singer or dancer, or even just regular folk. This is not something that the church wants to hear, but even the preacher and those who sit in the congregation can be a JUMPOFF.

At eighteen, I'd dated a preacher, and of course it involved sex. I also learned that there are words used to judge a preacher who dates without being married, especially if that woman is spending nights at his place. I have heard people say, "That's a jack-legged preacher."

When the church folks pass judgment on the next person, it leaves that person to believe he or she has to live for the church instead of living life for himself or herself. Then too you live your life as one big lie.

I am not saying that everybody does it. I am not saying that most people will do it. However, I know my ex was on Sunday morning TV preaching to the congregation after we left his house together because I had stayed over on Saturday nights in his bed with him, having mad sex. So I'm just saying to the church folks, you all should stop with the judging thing, too.

There is no use getting irate about the reality of this subject. It makes no sense writing about something I know of so well if I'm not going to give it to you straight up. Hot or cold, big or bold, it is what it is, and it was what it was.

Now, there is factual evidence that some pathetic bosses in the corporate world do cross the line and make it known that you have to JUMPOFF the top dog in order to move up or get the position you dream of having.

I worked short-term in the corporate field once and had a boss who told me that all I had to do was look good to keep my job. I used it to my advantage. I wore the shortest skirts I could find, so when I took a file into his office, he could damn near see my ass if I had to pick up something off the floor.

The female V.P. did complain, but I didn't care because I knew as long as I gave the boss what he wanted, I was secure. I was able to take 2-hour lunches because I gave him what the hell he wanted, which was to see my legs, and I got what I needed, too.

For those of you petrified of being a JUMPOFF, ask the person you want to get with if they have a significant other, instead of assuming they are single. Some men will not volunteer the information that they are already in a relationship. This is why I say to the wives and the girlfriends who play housewives, do not always hate on the JUMPOFFS. So I ask the real wives and play housewives, why take yourself through the possibility of accumulating health issues and getting wrinkles to set in around your forehead and under your eyes because you are stressed over your man and his JUMPOFF? You know very well what you had before you were married to him, so his behavior should be nothing new to you.

At the end of the day, as long as he is taking care

of you and paying those luxury, high-priced bills, as I said before, let Joe be Joe. You cannot tell a grown man what to do, and if a man wants to do it, you better believe he will find a way to do whatever he wants to do. JUMPOFFS aren't going anywhere. When one is gone, another one comes along, so until your so-called man or husband matures enough to stay away from JUMPOFFS, you will continue to be involved in drama.

The focal point of this book is to open up the minds of individuals (to let you know about JUMPOFFS.) I am only writing the story of my life, and what makes my life so interesting is the fact that I have had JUMPOFF experiences with some well-known people, whether I was the JUMPOFF, or they were my JUMPOFF.

Face the fact that most female JUMPOFFS do hold the power between the thighs. Then again, nowadays things are sort of different. My gay friend seemed to have more JUMPOFF experiences than I did.

So as we get into the story of my life, please know that not by any means am I trying to tell you how you should live your life. If you are a JUMPOFF or if you have a JUMPOFF, it is your life and you have to live it. I can only share with you my life experiences, and hopefully you will gather some insight on how things truly are in this world.

Moving forward, I will reveal to you what it was like dating Robert Kelly before the world knew him as R. Kelly. You will know how he made me feel and why we were each other's JUMPOFF.

Then there was a moment with Martin Lawrence. If Martin was in a relationship, I didn't know about it. Would I meet Martin and continue where we left off? Yes, I would.

Then my dealings with Suge were different. People would still ask me today, "What was it like to date Suge?" My answer to that is "Preparation; take the good with the bad. He's a man, not a monster."

Then my friend Tupac, R.I.P., was a clever

sweetheart. The Tupac I saw in interviews wasn't the Tupac I knew and lived with. He had a dear, soft spot that the world knew nothing about, unless you knew him.

Then I had a 6-year relationship with the ladies' man, Mr. Robert Jackson, who is married now to a very unattractive woman. (I mean, I want to believe she is a woman. I do have a friend who is a TS with a striking resemblance.) He wasn't even a celebrity, but he had more JUMPOFFS than George Clooney.

Later, I went out with producer Jazze Pha. Butterball Turkey is the name that only I used with him. I tried to be his JUMPOFF, but obstacles got in the way of that happening.

And sexy, only with his hat on, raspy voice Young Jeezy. We worked with the same producer, and I did a song with him. He is definitely one of the coolest guys I've ever met and hung out with.

Also, I had a crush on Shawty Redd, the producer of my single, "White Tee Girl Version," and would still jump him off today.

There were also other well-known people who were a part of my life, and as you read on, you'll see how my life tied in with the JUMPOFF world with them. So kick back and relax, because my real life story is about to start.

5

CATCHING THE VIBE WITH R. KELLY

I remember my life from the time I was 8 years old until now. Since I was a tomboy growing up, whenever I fought with a boy, it felt like the right thing to do. These days one would call it a "girl crush" on a boy, but I can assure you it was nothing like that at all for me.

In grammar school, I met a girl named Cassandra

who was a real tomboy and a bully. Everyone called her Katt. She picked on me so much during and after school that I got tired of it and wanted to show her the other tomboy who knew how to kick butt, and that person happened to be me. So one day after school, I did just that, kicked her butt, and a few days later she and I became friends. It really is true that when you kick a bully's butt they become cool with you.

Katt and I grew out of touch with each other for some years, even though she lived only two blocks from my parents at the time. It was years before we met up again as young ladies. Katt taught me a lot about men, how to hustle, and how to make real good money.

Katt became a regular stripper for a traveling strip team of girls called "The Kitty Kats," a traveling group founded in a hood club in Chicago. She is the reason R. Kelly and I met in the first place.

Because she had been stripping for a few years and knew how to hustle so well, it was quite easy for her to grab the attention of all types of men. The provocative attire she wore all the time helped to allure the men as well.

It all started one night when Katt wanted to go downtown Chicago to meet R. Kelly. She knew his hangout spot, and I was down for it. So we drove downtown to Rock 'n' Roll McDonald's, and sure enough Kelly was there.

As we drove closer, I saw Kelly leaning against his car along with a group of guys with a couple of females talking to them. After we parked and got out of the car, Katt tucked her stomach in so tight, she could barely breathe. I knew of Kelly; I had heard very little about him, but I didn't have the itch for him.

Kelly stared as we walked inside of McDonald's to order some food. Still I had no intention of trying to get his attention because I thought he was just okay-looking. Katt liked him and wanted to know him because he was popular, not to mention she thought he was fine.

As we were standing in line to order food, Katt watched Kelly walk through the door and gave me the signal he was coming in. Well, Kelly did speak, but he really didn't notice her. He was bold enough to come up to me, even though others were standing in the same line to order their food. I kindly introduced myself to him, and I introduced Katt to him. If looks could kill, he would have been dead that night because jealousy had fallen all over her face. Katt wanted him bad, and after she realized he had no interest in her, she pretended as if he was nothing then.

Kelly paid the little 3 dollars and something for my meal and asked if we could get together sometime.

At that point, I was more interested in him because Katt thought she was the trophy winner in all of the men.

It was a little noisy where we were standing, so we went outside to talk. The first thing I thought when we approached his black Mercedes was, he just wanted to show off his car. Little did he know, I was used to dealing with guys with BMWs and Mercedes, so I wasn't too impressed that he could afford a nice car.

In that same moment, he leaned against his car and grabbed my hands. I didn't mind the compliments he felt the urge to give me. Neither did I mind him coming on to me so soon and so strong, even though we had just met.

He must have picked up on my body language and figured that I still wasn't happy-go-lucky over him. So he made it known to me he was a singer with a number one song out on the radio and asked me to come out so I could see him perform with his group at the Cotton Club that following week.

I wasn't trying to be funny or anything. It's just that I wasn't star-struck. I figured I would catch his video when it came on the video channel. A few minutes more into the conversation, it was all about him and his video.

What caught my attention was, I brushed up against him and felt something long down below his waist. Funny, but my imagination ran wild. He moved so fast, we almost kissed that night. A few minutes later, my tongue would have been locked with his.

Katt comes out of McDonald's and halts the little connection Kelly was trying to establish with me. I rushed my conversation with Kelly because she suddenly was in a hurry to get back to her place. Kelly wanted me to stay and hang out with him and even offered to take me home, but I couldn't stay because at the time Katt didn't know how to drive.

It was all good. We got back in the car and left. Katt made it a point to tell me that Kelly was a freak and is known to mess with a lot of girls. That didn't stop me from wanting to get together with him. I was hoping he would call me so I could see how big a freak he was. I remember going home that night and turning the TV on to catch his video late that night, but I fell asleep.

He never did call me, so I finally called him, and we talked. Kelly was the more vocal one, and I just pretty much listened. He claimed he was so happy I called because he had lost my number. That wasn't it. He had gotten so many phone numbers from different girls, he didn't have time to write my name by my number. Boy, dealing with Kelly, a fast mover, you better learn the game quick is all I can say.

I was inquisitive about his music, that he invited me to the studio for one of his sessions. Since Battery Recording Studio was out of the way from where I needed to go, I told him that maybe another time I could come and watch. I was excited about meeting him and going out with him, but he didn't need to know that.

The next day he picked me up, and we went out to eat at a soul food place. I learned a lot more about him as we laughed and talked. He was fun to talk to because he had a great sense of humor. As matter of fact, from the time I knew Kelly, I don't remember one time where he caught an attitude about anything. He always seemed happy with life.

By midnight, we were both tired, and he asked

me to come back to his place. I knew I would drop my panties to this guy quick if I went to his place, so I held out that night, too. If I had gone to his place, it would have been on and popping.

I wanted more than just that moment with him, and with all the girls he had at the time, I didn't want to be the one forgotten about after one night. I wanted to have sex with him on my time because at the end of the day, he would still have plenty women knocking his drawers off, so knocking me off was like a piece of cake to him. But I wanted to make him wait to eat this cake I had to offer.

The restaurant had already closed, and we both ignored the fact that it was late. But the owner didn't mind. He knew Kelly, so he kept the doors open for him any time he wanted to be there.

Somehow, the subject of sex came up, and as we talked about it more, I got moist and hot. So the next thing I did was the touch-and-feel test. That way I could get somewhat of an idea of what a guy is working with. Sometimes, it could be hard to tell what a guy is working with if his jeans were loose. That's why I love sweat pants. When a guy gets hard, it's easier to feel the true size of his dome.

I didn't have to ask Kelly if I could feel his dome. He grabbed my right hand and placed it there. Then we kissed. I wanted to suck on it right then, but I decided to spare the owner and the cook a free show that night. He tried talking me into going home with him the entire time we sat there. I didn't make it any easier, unzipping his pants and stroking his dome. The feel of it was nice. I imagined having sex with him right then.

A part of me felt guilty because I was going out with a preacher guy at the time, so I tried to hold back on screwing around with Kelly. The preacher guy was a freak also, but I was young and hot, and wanted more to bargain with.

Finally, around 2 in the morning, we left the restaurant and went our separate ways. I can still remember how Kelly's dome stuck out of his jeans, and it was big and hard.

A few days had passed and I hadn't heard from him. You know someone has another person in their life when they are not quick at calling you the day after to hang out again. I thought about him, but I wasn't going to sweat him.

When he did call me, I wasn't home, but my little sister answered the phone. R. Kelly was such a big flirt, he asked my sister how old she was. My sister was only 13 at the time, but she pretended to be 15. He also made it a point to tell her who he was, probably expecting her to jump and scream.

He asked her if she looked like me, if she went out. Since then, she has been a fan of his, just from his short conversation with her that day.

Moments later, my sister called to tell me Kelly had called looking for me, and she told me what he'd asked her. She was excited to hear R. Kelly's voice, but she'd downplayed it to him like, "Oh, okay, I will tell her you called."

But I didn't get why he even felt the need to carry on a conversation with her, whether long or short. None of my male friends had ever said hi to my little sister.

Anyway, I called him back, and we met up again. It was still on my mind to ask him about the phone conversation with my little sister. He tried to smooth it over, saying, she sounded like me on the phone. I thought to myself, *Okay, brother, if you say so.* I didn't believe him, so I let it go. I think I was more into screwing him that night than anything else. That part with my sister almost blew it, but after a few drinks with him I had long forgotten.

His loft was nice and inviting. I wore a short skirt with no panties on that night. I wanted him to know I was ready for whatever. He had an open bottle of liquor with some music playing and no bed at the time. So he set up shop on the floor.

Kelly wore shorts that night, and when he sat on the floor, all I saw was his nuts hanging out from the side of his shorts. It looked good! I wanted him to sex me right then. I imagined him taking control and pounding me doggie-style.

I wanted to feel that! My mind started to wonder if he was the man to lay it on me real good or if the look was deceiving and I would be disappointed.

He knew his dome was hanging from his shorts, and when I assured him it was, he pulled his shorts down and leaned back on the floor. It was nicer than I thought, once it was all the way hard. I got closer to him and stroked him while he gently rubbed my kitty. I got on top of him and grinded as my kitty moved up and down his dome.

My first night with Kelly was a night to remember. He was freaky! I sat on his face, and he asked me to do a golden shower on him. I smiled and told him that wasn't my thing. I asked him if he ever had it done, and he said once. He was sexy and all, but I couldn't bring myself to urinate on his face. It was our first time together and what might have been sexy and freaky to him was not sexy and freaky to me. Golden showers are not sexy to me at all. It wasn't then, and still isn't today.

However, he did use his tongue to satisfy a girl. I liked how he kissed as well. His tongue was deep inside my mouth, and I was dripping wet by then. I remember more of the foreplay between us than the actual intercourse. Once he got it inside of me, it took him all of 5 minutes to release. I did enjoy the strength he had to go a second time around.

After it was over, we sat up, had more to drink, and talked for a while. He asked me to stay the night with him, and I did. He told me how music made him feel sexy and good. His love for music was the same love he had for sex.

I'd never asked him if he was involved in a relationship at the time because I figured, what sense does it make to ask him, knowing he probably has sex with different girls all the time? At any rate we used protection, so it didn't matter. My girl had already told me how freaky he was, so I had to see for myself. I thought, *Who could be freakier than my preacher boyfriend?*

Kelly's relationship with me was more about sex than anything, though sometimes we talked about music and other things dealing with the entertainment business. I was also interested in him because he was in the music business and I wanted to get my foot in the door. He could have screwed 50 women for all I cared. I love a man who really enjoys the moment of pure pleasure, not someone who just wants to stick it in you and don't think about pleasing the woman. A man who thinks about his lady is sexier than a man who just wants to explode as soon as he gets inside of you.

At the time I was involved with Kelly, I had no idea he would be looked at as a sex symbol. Truly, I had a nice time with him.

He also had other weird moments and fetishes, like having sex with pregnant women because their kitty is always wet. I found him to be down-to-earth and extremely talented.

Kelly was the first person who told me that I would need an open mind towards sex in the entertainment business.

Before the end of the night, I knew all about his sexual encounter with an older female executive. I was surprised he told me that much, but he had no shame.

Throughout the short-term relationship I had with Kelly, I learned a lot about the entertainment business. I was surprised to learn that you had to treat sex as your product. Not so much for money, but whatever. So to that person who came up with the slogan sex sells, you are right on the money.

That brings me back to the notion that JUMPOFFS are necessary and will always be around. Sex not only sells, but it plays a major role in entertainment.

Rappers are a prime example of it with their videos. If the girl isn't half naked with butt shots, she ain't getting in. No one can convince me otherwise. There are a lot of people in denial, but once you get in the business, you get to see for yourself.

Everything Kelly schooled me on came from his manager, who schooled him on how to react to sex in the business. I talked to his manager at the time on the phone once, and he put me in the mind of a freak himself. The first thing he said was, "Rob told me you look good, so he has to bring you to see me in Woodland Hills." Well, I never saw the manager.

The relationship between Kelly and I did not last that long. I did like him, but at the time, his lifestyle was a lot faster than mine. It was a bit much for me to understand how the music business will take all morals from you if you let it, and that most people would go for it because the lifestyle is great. The fame is addictive, and they want to be rich and famous.

We talked about how he would always get that feeling; that one day he would be musically famous. After a while, the conversation became short with us because there was nothing else to talk about. We enjoyed each other for sex, and that's pretty much what it was all about.

He did say he would help me get in the music business, but that never happened. But you could say anything to a young, naïve girl like I was then, and she would believe. Some guys will say whatever to keep hitting the panties.

Weeks later, our time spent with each other was shortened. Late nights I would visit him at the studio, and there would be younger girls than me hanging around. Kelly's friend Rocky sold him out by telling his business about him and the girls at the studio. I felt it was his life. Whatever decisions he made, he had to deal with them. I recognized his issues; it didn't take a rocket scientist to figure him out at all.

By then I started having a very heavy schedule myself. One day he called me up to chill with him at the studio, and I did. I met Wayne Williams that day, a DJ from Chicago who now works with J Records. Wayne and I listened as R. Kelly played one of his songs on the piano.

Sure enough, when Wayne left the studio, Kelly couldn't keep his hands off me. He asked me to bend over for him, and I did. We ended up having sex again that night.

I told him he was sexy and talented and made me

feel good sexually. I got plenty of foreplay from him, but I really didn't need it to get super wet and hot for him. He would take his big black thing out and rub it against my kitty, and it was over. I had to get my time in with him when I could.

I must say that Kelly was one JUMPOFF to remember, whether I was his or he was mine, I enjoyed the moments we did share together. That night was just as good as the first night we had sex together.

I gave him what he wanted, he gave me what I needed. I remember asking him if I could write him a song. He was all for it, but I had to be prepared to sing it to him instead of writing it down because he didn't write songs down. I never thought anything of it when he told me he had people write his songs down for him. Then I found out, through a person who was no longer friends with him, that he had a problem reading well.

This former friend of Kelly's threw him under the bus and told me a lot of foul things about him. But it was his words, and not words spoken by Kelly, so none of that mattered to me. I thought it was bad for him and Kelly to be friends for years and then break up over some chick, but I guess that is the power of the kitty.

I then went on a production stage play tour across the county, so I was no longer in contact with Kelly.

A few years later, he started working with Aaliyah. By that time, my girlfriend Oobie was friends with him.

After the controversy between him and Aaliyah, he later got married again, and no one knew about it. Kelly didn't tell anyone he was married. When I saw his wife at the studio one time, I thought it was a joke. I thought people were just saying he was married, because she would never act like he was her husband. They would never leave together or nothing. No contact whatsoever. She wasn't pleasing to the eyes, so I figured she must have been his fallback.

A few years later I felt like the fame had gotten to his head because he had fallen out with the majority of his friends and walked around as if he didn't care. It never bothered me that his head was big. I was happy for any success that crossed his path.

When I found out Kelly was married, I wasn't trying to see him again. I went on with life as if I never knew him.

Overall, my life with R. Kelly was cool. It was fun, and I learned a lot from him, and I have always wished him the best in his career because he does have a caring heart.

6

WELCOME TO THE STRIPPER WORLD

I started hanging out with my girlfriend Katt more, the same girl I beat up in school and through whom I met R. Kelly. She was a dancer for the female strippers called The Kitty Kats. This club we hung out at; had hoochie mommas, drug dealers, and pimps. Out in public, Katt would dress no different than if she was doing a show on stage. I'm not a jealous person, nor am I a hater, so I liked how she dressed. It was interesting and fun to look at.

We know looks could be deceiving, but with Katt there was no deception on her part. What you saw, you did get.

I have always found strippers to be sexy. You might hear some people say that strippers have low self-esteem. Call it what you want, but I say the smart ones get paid.

I got caught up with hanging out with Katt in the stripper world. I would go and watch her shows from time to time. Girls got down on the floor, and the guys would lick their kitties.

Katt was good at stripping, and she made good money. She did not play that "little money" stuff. In fact, little money didn't fit in her vocabulary, so she said. That weekend, she invited me to a private party where she was hired to dance at for some white guys.

Katt had me believing she made good money.

She had already been dancing for a few years, so I told her I wouldn't mind trying it one day.

Another party came up the following weekend. I asked her if she ever had to perform sexual favors at these parties. She claimed that the guys would never have sex with her at these parties or even touch her. But I clearly remembered a man licking her kitty when she sat on top of his face one night while she was busting it wide open. So that was lie number one out of her mouth.

Bottom line is, she wanted to be a high-priced stripper. I did like her a lot and thought she had a lot of sophistication.

The only tacky thing on her was her hair weave. I thought everything else was in place. I mean, I have bad days too with hair weave, but this was the worst I can remember from someone I know personally.

One day, she called to ask me if I would go over to some guy's house with her. Supposedly, she'd met this guy at that same tacky strip club where she danced at. He was a so-called film producer or director wanting to film a nude scene with two girls who had to pretend to be lesbians. He claimed he was going to pay each person five thousand dollars.

Now this is where I learned my lesson. He didn't tell me he would give us five thousand dollars each. He'd had this talk with Katt, who said not to worry about it because she trusted this guy. I thought it was cool because she talked a good game as if she was really the money girl. Boy, was I wrong.

Once we made it to this guy's place, the scenery did not feel right. He introduced himself as Will. He tried his best to sound like a real honest dude. It was my first time doing something like this, so I didn't know what to expect.

Will had a camera sitting on the dolly, and lights were set up as if he really knew what he was doing, but he had no TV monitor. What bothered me was, he lived in a cheap apartment.

Now as I look back on that part of my life, I have to remind myself that I never rode that short yellow school bus. So it had to be my youth that would explain why I was so dumb to believe some stranger would pay us to pretend we were lesbians, and get naked for the camera. I'm so glad wisdom has been good to me; otherwise I would still be a dummy today. I guess that's all a part of being young and growing up. Not much gets past me these days.

Once the clothes came off and his little camera started rolling, it was my turn to pretend I was licking Katt's kitty. I smelled something foul. It smelled like a bucket of crab legs down there. I almost threw up. I tried holding my breath, but I could only do that for so long.

In my mind, this was not happening at all. I couldn't go on pretending this act of having my face that close to that odor in her kitty was okay.

However, that was simple compared to what happened next. This guy put you in the mind of JJ from the TV series *Good Times*. I saw him climbing his tall, skinny behind up in the bed to position his camera. At that point I used my hair to cover my face because there was already a lack of trust, and I didn't know this guy.

Next, he started to tongue-kiss Katt. I moved over and got out of the bed. I pretended to go and get something to drink and picked up my clothes. As I was leaving the room, I saw him moving down toward Katt's kitty, using his mouth. How gross of him to not be bothered by that foul odor!

I left out of the room and changed into my clothes. By the time I made it back in the bedroom, Will was having unprotected sex with Katt while the camera was still rolling. No one had told me that having real sex was part of the plan. He did have a big monster though.

Katt gave me the eye as she made these crazy sex noises, pretending the sex was good. I was a little pissed because she was always the first one to say that she never had sex with tricks without protection. The first thing I thought about was, this guy probably does this to a lot of girls.

No matter what this guy told her, he hadn't paid

us one red cent yet, and she let him do all of that to her… after meeting him at that nasty club. What was she thinking? I thought she was much smarter than that, with all the crap she talked. Later I found out that he had told her he would give her extra money for having sex with him for the camera.

She seemed a little disturbed after he finished screwing her, by that time I had already gotten dressed. She was probably embarrassed and wondering what my thoughts were.

What made it even worse was, he didn't pay us as he'd promised. Instead, he gave us two personal checks and said to wait three days before cashing it. If looks could kill, he would have been a dead duck. After he said to wait before we cashed the checks, Katt's face turned red, and her whole expression changed. I guess he thought we were dummies to believe he would have the money after we left his cheesy apartment.

Katt was furious, but she smiled as if everything was good. The whole day she used every curse name she could find for this guy who pranked us. In the first place, we should have gotten half of that money up front. It didn't bother me too much, knowing we had been pranked. But I can understand why Katt was so upset. Hell, if I'd had unprotected sex with the guy, I would have been pissed at myself too.

After a while, I began to think it was funny. She thought she was the queen of taking tricks' money, but he'd swindled us.

Katt looked real crazy to only dance for white guys at private parties, but then let this black guy screw her out of five thousand dollars. I say there is a bigger city slicker for every slicker. I sure learned my lesson, because we never got paid, even after all the threats Katt made to this man.

After all the visits we paid him, he just stopped answering his phone and the door after so long. Then the last time we went to his house, he threatened to call the police if we showed up again at his door.

One thing I told her was, I would have to get

paid first before I do anything. From then on, whenever Katt arranged something for us that involved money, I had no problems with it. She made sure the money was given to us first, and the money was always good.

So I was officially caught up and introduced to the world of sex and money. Katt taught me that sex sells. Kelly taught me to treat sex as if it was a product. Good or bad, it was my life.

It didn't stop there. I enjoyed getting money that was easy to come by. In my mind, I was like, you give me what I want and you can enjoy all you want with me.

I was young and had a lot to offer. Still I had a lot of growing to do. I had to be tough with guys and carry that "didn't-give-a-damn" attitude.

Instead of me being a bitch, I made a guy into a bitch first. If I heard a guy saying something like, "I fucked that bitch," and it was directed toward me, I didn't care because, believe me, if they had been with me, then it cost them some pretty good change.

When I was young, I was into dating street guys like drug dealers and hustlers. They'd taught me the streets, and how to have a JUMPOFF and not care what anyone says.

One day I was at the hotel with one of my homeboys just hanging out, having fun. Two of his friends came through with weed and drinks. One of his friend's name Angel made it known that she was a dancer at a very exclusive strip club with a white clientele, where the money was good and easy to make.

A few days later, I went to check out the club. This place was a hole-in-the-wall joint with plenty of money rolling through. The reason only white men came through was because the owner was a racist Italian who hated black men. There was a lot going on in that club, which was more like a strip club in the front with the sex rooms in the back, along with the VIP area. Hell, it damn near was like a cathouse.

My first day at work wasn't bad. The girls helped

me out with what to do, what not to do, and who not to trust. They didn't have to tell me because I didn't trust any of them. I was only there for one reason— to get my money.

The old Italian owner looked like the man from the movie *Sugar Hill*, and his name was Gus too. All I knew was, his old Italian tail was screwing one of the girls there who walked around as if she was "Miss It," and she was not. I called her Miss Sloppy because that best described her body.

The money was good at this club. I tried to take every dime and dollar those white boys came through with. Some were married, and I tried to take every dime they had, too. I am sure those wives had no idea where their husbands were.

A few days later, I called up Katt and told her about the place. I wanted to turn her on to some club money that had white clients, instead of that hole-in-the-wall place. I never understood how someone could dance in a hole-in-the-wall place but then tell me they only dance for white men on the outside of the club. Why waste your time? Keep it consistent.

Katt claimed she was making about two thousand a week doing private parties. If that was true, she wouldn't have been so glad to get to the club I was at. She came to the club, and Gus hired her on the spot as well. It reminded me of the scene in *The Players Club* when Ebony was hired on the spot.

She came in telling the girls we were cousins. The girls would call us men, because we both had banging bodies. They were all jealous because we took their clients from them, but you cannot blame the dancer. Men want to pay for what's hot, and we happened to be hotter than every girl in the club.

After 2 months, I was tired of working at that club. I didn't want to get caught up into dancing and do nothing else, so I quit, but Katt continued to work there. Making thousands for me and millions for others wasn't my cup of tea. I thought it was time for me to step it up a few notches.

The goal I had set for myself was to be an actress and to be surrounded by entertainers in music and film, not to be in the stripper world, or dealing with dumb girls who took their money home to their pimps.

7

BEAUTY SHOP PART 2 TOUR

Over at Lilly's Talent Agency, I got myself a casting agent so I could go out to auditions as a professional actress. It just so happened that I was listening to the radio one day and heard an announcement that Shelly Garrett was coming to town to hold auditions for his next tour.

In March, I went to a Shelly Garrett's casting in Chicago for his play, called *Beauty Shop Part 2*. I told Katt about the audition, and she met me at McCormick Place to audition. A lot of people were there in line to audition for different roles.

When it was our turn, we went into the camera room together. Already, we knew what routine we were going to do. Shelly and his crew sat at the opposite end of the table while the camera guy filmed us. After the audition, Shelly gave us a big smile and said, "Very well." We left them with all of our contact numbers and felt good about the audition. It was the first time I had gone on such a big audition for a major theater play.

Later, I was given a role in an independent film called *Scandals*, which is how I met Mel Jackson, the guy who got his stardom playing Samuel in the movie *Soul Food*. He was Big Manny, the boyfriend of my character, in the film *Scandals*. Mel was just a friend and a nice guy. At the time he stayed from house to house and didn't have a car, so I would pick him up sometimes and drop him off after filming.

Katt and I were still hanging out together. I was trying to get him to date Katt at the time because she liked light-skinned pretty boys, while I liked dark-skinned big-lipped boys. Although he looked good, Katt was never interested. She was all about men with money, and he didn't have anything to offer her at the time. He was just a struggling actor who was too cute and had the potential to be a little too soft for my taste. I knew he had a crush on me, because he said so.

His two roommates, Jarquo and Patrick, were part of the cast as well, good-looking guys all brighter than the sun. Jarquo was the only one who didn't seem to have "a little sweetness in his pants" in him.

Patrick later played a role in the HBO series, *Six Feet Under*. We all know that series was about queers. There were rumors going around that Patrick was sleeping with *Ladies of Englewood* director, Kim. That was after he landed his role as T-Bone in the film. The rumors were found to be true because while he was contracted as a cast member on the soap opera *All My Children* in New York, Kim had him served with paternity papers on the set.

I kept in contact with him for a short while, and

although I knew about him and Kim's sex quarrel, I never mentioned it until he told me. He said it was no rumor, and that it was true. He was her JUMPOFF, because Kim was married at the time.

During this time of filming those two independent films, I hadn't heard anything back from Shelly Garrett. Then July rolled around, and I finally got the call from Shelly Garrett himself. He hired me to be a part of the cast of *Beauty Shop Part 2*. I had to pay my own way to California and get there in two days.

Katt was casted in the play as well, so I booked our plane tickets at the same time.

When we arrived at the airport, Xavier and Shelly's bodyguard were waiting inside of the airport for us. About 5 of us had flown in from Chicago for this production. The first stop was Shelly's house near Diamond Bar, California. We took the role as dancers along with 3 other girls from Chicago.

The only girl he cast from Chicago as a main character was Kendra Meeks, now known as Kendra

Davis, wife of Antonio Davis, who played in the NBA with the Indiana Pacers.

Kendra also appeared on *The Real Housewives of Atlanta* as Kim's interior designer. She's also the owner of that fabulous home in Roswell, Georgia. Kendra played the role of Mercedes. She was only 18 at the time, but she seemed mature. We were the two youngest cast members, besides Shelly's daughter, who also had a role in the show.

Later that night, the cast checked into the hotel not far from Shelly's house.

Rehearsal began the next day at Shelly's house, where everyone introduced themselves and told what role they would be playing.

Shelly was rumored to be the touchy type to the ladies he cast. When I was alone with him to collect my weekly wage, I told him I wasn't there for anything, other than to do my job. Of course, he took offense because, after that day, he had little to do with me. That's why it isn't good to go with rumors about a person before you get to know them yourself.

After 2 long sweaty weeks of rehearsal, it was time to head to San Diego, California for our first big show. *Beauty Shop Part 2* was a sold-out show every single night, and we were all excited to hear that. This was my official entry into the entertainment world.

Everything I had learned from Kelly, and my street knowledge, I had to remember to carry with me always. Katt and I were roommates in San Diego, and we always talked about sticking together, but that was a lie for the second time with her. She was all for herself. She wanted to make sure I didn't get Shelly Garrett's attention because she wanted him.

Things really changed between us by the time we started touring. Throughout the journey from San Diego, California to Milwaukee, Wisconsin, she stayed on Shelly's coach with him, and there was only one bed on that coach. I can't say what went on while she spent that time on his coach, but we all knew the deal.

After a few years, I finally learned she was a

jealous person and thought she was the more attractive one, that she should be the one guys should flock to instead of me, but it was totally the opposite. Clearly you can see that her looks are not her best assets. She did have a nice body, but that was all she had to offer.

By the time we made it to Wisconsin, Shelly put her ass off his coach. She looked dumb. What she didn't realize was, I wasn't attracted to him at all. He was a nice-looking older man, but he wasn't my type. He reminded me of my father at the time.

All I could think about was, you were stupid with the porno guy, and now you are just as stupid with Shelly. By the time we arrived in the next city I requested a different roommate and wanted nothing else to do with her.

I saw her for the trick she was at the time and realized we could never be real friends. She never was a true friend, and I should have known that back in Chicago from the first time she acted up because

Kelly wanted me and not her. She always wanted to eat the tail of the lobster and give me the legs with little or no meat on it. I had to solve that problem by getting another roommate. My roommate was immediately changed, and she and I never spoke to each other the rest of the tour.

So during the course of the tour Shelly and Kendra Davis started dating after he threw Katt in the trash and canned her. Shelly was raw; I have to give it to him for being a mad player back then. It seemed as if he had more whores than Don Juan.

I remember he had all types of pretty women meeting him in different states. He was doing it just like the NBA players, with a different chick in every city. He even had his baby momma on tour with us as head of wardrobe. He kept his women close, and if they kept their mouth shut about the next one, he would keep them around longer. If they troubled him about the other woman, they would get the boot.

Kendra knew the ropes. She knew her position and would always refer to Shelly as "Daddy." There were times Ms. Kendra did get jealous and throw a dramatic fit. All the same I liked the fire in her. We all knew when Kendra and Shelly got into it because he would put her off his coach for the next ride and put her on the cast coach.

Kendra and I did become friends. She was sweet, but given the chance she would cut your throat also. I liked her though; even though she would snitch on the cast and tell Shelly a lot of things that went on. I knew what she was all about, so her ways never bothered me. Smart-mouth Kendra was the name the cast had for her.

Shelly was a pro at what he did with women. Brother had good game now.

The violence in their relationship became noticeable when Shelly met Melissa Morgan and started dating her. The entire cast was shocked when we saw him with Melissa because Shelly would only date light-skinned girls out in public, and she was darker than most of his other women.

One day Shelly and Kendra got into a heated argument backstage, and she did not go out on stage. That left Shelly with forcing Kendra's understudy on stage with little notice.

Big Mike, aka Michael Clarke Duncan, was part of the cast as Shelly's bodyguard and sometimes guarded the cast. Shelly had Big Mike guard Kendra to make sure she didn't ruin his show that night. Kendra was so fiery at the time, if you pissed her off, there was no telling what she would do, sort of like what she is all about now.

Still she was cool. She just had a big mouth and never bothered anybody unless they looked at her the wrong way. I thought she was hilarious most of the time.

That was an awful night to remember. The understudy screwed up so bad, the cast had to lead her with her lines. I called that night of the show a circus night because it really did feel like that. During the intermission, she cried the whole time and told everyone Shelly had jumped on her because she no longer wanted to be with him because he was an old violent man. Well, this man was the same person she referred to as Daddy. So how awkward was that of her?

Whether it was true about him putting bruises on her or not, the cast never believed her. We knew the argument had something to do with Melissa being backstage that night. I was surprised Kendra acted that way because she had been Shelly's JUMPOFF since he threw Katt in the trash can.

We saw more of Melissa, who stayed locked on Shelly's arms. A few months later, the two of them were married.

I got a good laugh out of it, not because he sent Kendra home, but as soon as Katt found out, she thought she had a chance to slide back in with him. I believe it was the smell of her kitty that turned him off because he never wanted her again.

Katt did squeeze her way in closer to Shelly by dating his bisexual stylist. I guess, when you're desperate, you'll take anything. Burt's sexuality was no secret. Hell, when he walked, he switched better than Tyra Banks on a runway. I enjoyed the way he talked just as I enjoy my gay friends today.

8

MARTIN LAWRENCE GOODS

The tour went on, Kendra was replaced, and Shelly's relationship with Melissa was good.

Now it was time to get my JUMPOFF skills back in the mix. Things were getting boring for me, so I had to get something cranking.

I met Martin Lawrence at Radio City Music Hall in New York during his comedy tour. When I first saw Martin, I knew I was going to have him. After the show that night, I went back to my hotel room thinking, Martin was staring at me while I was sitting in that front row. But, hell, he was staring at everybody.

The following day Eddie Murphy and his beautiful wife Nicole came to the Beacon Theater to watch our show. Martin came that night also. Inside the dressing room, all of the girls talked about who would get Martin. He was funny, short, and hilarious to watch on stage.

I got a chance to meet Eddie backstage before he went into the audience and joined his beautiful wife. But they ended up leaving early because she was pregnant at the time and was having labor contractions.

After the show, the cast took pictures with Martin, who I thought was even cuter in person than he was on TV. All the girls in the cast were on him like maggots. Everyone wanted a picture with him.

When it was my turn to take a picture with

Martin, I shook his hands and slid him my hotel phone number inside of a piece of paper. He laughed as he held on to it. I didn't have a cell phone at the time, so Martin called my hotel room later that night and asked if he could send his driver to pick me up.

When I arrived at The Mark hotel, where Martin was staying, I was high off shots of vodka. I had not been with a celebrity since R. Kelly.

Martin's hotel suite rocked. I was good and lit from the vodka, and he looked better at that moment than he did earlier. We laughed and talked for a while.

When I drink liquor, it has a great effect on my bladder, so I was back and forth to the bathroom.

Martin had gotten so comfortable with my conversation with him. He took his shirt off, and his chest looked like a little boy's chest. He was much sexier with his shirt on than he was with it off. I had to constantly tell myself, "This is Martin, a grown man that I came over to JUMPOFF, not a little boy."

He thought I was a little nervous or shy, so he tried his best to make me feel comfortable. I went to use the bathroom again, but this time when I came out, he had already dimmed the lights. At that moment, I knew he had the same thing on his mind that I had on my mine.

He knew what time it was when I'd agreed to go over to his hotel room at 1:00 A.M.. After all, I had pursued him the night of the show. He didn't give me his number, I gave him mine.

I did the obligatory "penis check," taking my hands and rubbing him inside of his pants to get a good feel and a smell too, since I was going there. Now I know some guys are small if they're not all the way hard, but once it becomes hard, that thing could possibly hang to the floor. Well, after a few minutes of trying and kissing, it didn't seem to grow.

He said he was excited because I was so beautiful, that he gets nervous around beautiful women. Okay, I can see a guy being nervous the first time with a new girl when he doesn't get it that much. At the time, he was a big-name person, so any woman would still have loved to be where I was at.

I wanted to go all the way with him that night. He had me hot just kissing on my body. He pulled my panties off with his teeth, tossed his head over to the side, and blew it out of his mouth. And he made this roaring sound when he did it.

I laughed so hard. I called him the wild kingdom animal because no one had ever done that. In the middle of our romance, he was still being a comic.

I leaned back on the couch, spread my legs while he kissed my thighs, and let him eat his cake and have his ice cream, too. After a while, I had to pull him up because he was working my kitty like a workaholic. It felt good, but I started to feel numb.

I enjoyed the night, and I thought it was well worth it. He'd pleased me enough with his tongue. So who can complain? I didn't need the penetration.

He asked me to stay the night, but I turned down

the offer. I had to be at a curtain call at 6:15 A.M., and didn't want to look lazy in rehearsal, so I called it a night between us and had his driver drop me back off at the hotel we were staying at.

Martin was so popular at the time, he could've had any girl he wanted too, but he chose me, and I chose to have him as my JUMPOFF.

The next day came around, and he didn't call all morning. So I called his room and left him a message to call me back, but he never did. It was no big deal, nor were there any hard feelings. I never heard from Martin and his cute banana penis again.

Somehow, the next day, word got back to Shelly that I was out seeing Martin at his hotel, and he didn't like that. I believe he was jealous because he had never spanked my booty. I was sure he thought I had given Martin some booty, which I would have, if only he could get it up. So I was called a groupie by Shelly Garrett.

We went word for word with one another. I knew what that was all about. Those funky girls were all jealous because Paula, my roommate, had told them that I went out with Martin, and it got back to Shelly. For the remainder of the tour, it seemed like Shelly picked on everything I was doing, especially with my performance. I felt harassed because I chose to see Martin Lawrence.

On the other hand, I didn't care what he felt. He wasn't my man, and maybe it was time for him to realize that he wasn't the only player in the crew. Then I thought to myself, *I wonder if I had been his little JUMPOFF for the day if he would have reacted that way toward me.*

That could have been dangerous. I know I am good at what I do and what I give. So if I'd had sex with him, he probably would have put his head through a brick wall. I know how to run circles when I want to.

Now that just goes to show you—If you don't have sex with directors or executives when they want, look out because your position is likely to be unstable.

I stayed with the tour a few more months before I decided to leave because Shelly and I were not getting along. I wasn't Kendra, nor was I screwing him, so there was no way he was going to tell me what I could or could not do. So I left the show a few months before the tour ended.

Months later, I called up my friend, Michael Clarke Duncan, who'd moved to California to pursue his acting career after the tour was over. Big Mike was so cute. He wanted me to live in Los Angeles bad. We talked a lot on the phone, and he finally told me he had a crush on me during the tour. I had tried to keep the conversation friendly, but he just let it out one day that he really was interested in me. I never knew he was digging me, so I had never looked at him in that way.

Big Mike was the bodyguard and my fitness trainer. So with all the huffing, puffing, and spreading my legs while making ugly faces, I had no idea he was paying attention to me. That was news for my ears, and it caught me by surprise. I was flattered, but he was just way too big.

I was curious to know how Shelly got wind of the little episode with Martin when we were on tour, and he said one of the girls told him. Big Mike also reminded me of that moment one day while on tour when he carried me to the room to lie down because I had a bad headache, something I had completely forgotten.

We had deep conversations about what he liked in a woman. Big Mike had a thing for women with pretty feet. At times he would give me phone sex and have me dripping wet. I had my reason for not screwing around with Big Mike. He was a sweetheart, but he was a friend for life.

When I met my girlfriend Lori in Los Angeles, he came over to her house. I went to one of Big Mike's auditions with him, and we later went out to eat.

Hollywood was good. Everybody wanted to be somebody.

A few days later, while I was in L.A., I went to Dr. Dre's audition for his video, "California," starring him and Tupac. There I met this girl named Casey, and for some reason we hit it off pretty well. She was a rapper, and so was I. I liked her West Coast flavor and sound. We exchanged phone numbers.

She told me she was from Chicago, and staying in California with her mom for a few months. She invited me to a studio she was recording at that same night. The producer she was working with had also worked with Dre on the NWA album. This guy gave us the ins and outs of the music business.

Apparently, the guy was digging Casey along with being a friend to her. I enjoyed being with Casey that night. She was pretty but tough, crazy, and fun to be around. She puzzled me because she was a proper rapper with no street knowledge but loved smoking weed.

I stayed at the studio a while with her and listened in on her session. Then I left for the night and went back to my folks' house I was staying at.

Early the next morning Casey called and asked me to hang out with her that day. Later that night, we went out to a comedy club called Fat Tuesday's, the happening spot at the time for all of the who's who. That night we went there, so many people were trying to get in, the bodyguard had the door on lockdown.

I spotted Damon Wayans and asked him if he could pretend we were with him just to get us inside. He was so cool. Though he didn't even know us, he let us grab him by the arms and he told the security we were with him, and they let us inside with no problem. How cool was that!

****

I thank Damon for getting us in that club because if it wasn't for him, I would have never met Suge or Tupac. Thank you, Damon Wayans.

9

DATING SUGE KNIGHT; THE DRAMA BEGINS

We walked into the crowded club and went and sat down right behind Tupac. I whispered in Casey's ear that Tupac was in front of us.

All this time Casey kept saying how she was going to meet Tupac and wanted to have sex with him. She wanted him to know that we were rappers too. She was hoping he would give us a shot and listen to us.

Naturally she was a fan of Tupac's. She tapped him on the shoulder and spoke to him. I asked him if we could see him when he gets a chance, so he got up from his seat right then and took us in the kitchen area of the club.

This big, tall, light-skinned guy followed us. At the time, I had no idea who he was. So when he got us in the back he asked us what did we want, and we told him that we rap. We did a little rap for him, and he liked it. He also liked our look. So he invited us to the studio and to hang out with them for that night. Then we left the kitchen area and went back out to catch the end of the comedy hour.

When the show was over with, Tupac and the Outlawz all left out in a rush, and they were rowdy too. They left out so fast, and it was so crowded, we lost him for a second. While we stood outside waiting to get a parking attendant to get Casey's car, we saw Tupac pull up in a drop-top Mercedes along with a Jeep carrying the Outlawz behind him.

That same big guy that was with Tupac was driving a red drop-top car and asked me to come to the car, which I did. He asked what were we about to do, and I told him we didn't have anything to do. So he asked us to come with them, because they were going to get something to eat.

I told him we had to wait on the car, and he said we could ride with them, to hop in to the Jeep behind him. That Jeep was full, so we hopped on the guys' lap, and they drove off real fast behind Tupac.

Tupac stopped his car as he was driving down Sunset Boulevard, got out in the middle of the street, and started dancing to one of his songs. Then he got back in the car and drove off real fast again.

We made it to the restaurant and had to go in through the back entrance. Tupac sat at a table with a girl sitting next to him. We didn't know where she came from, but she must have met him there.

It was late at night when we all ordered something to eat, and between all of us, we took up two tables. The big, tall, light-skinned guy who'd asked us to come with him and Tupac sat at the table with us.

Casey and I were quiet. A couple of the guys asked us to sing something for them, and I told them it was too late, that I had too much to drink. I ended up singing a happy birthday song, and it wasn't good at all. I wasn't the best singer, especially while drinking.

Then the big, tall guy asked us where we were from, and we told him Chicago, that we were trying to get a record deal and did not have a place to stay out in L.A. He said not to worry about it, that he would give us some place to stay and as long as we were willing to work, he didn't mind helping out. I thought, *Yeah, right. Whatever.* Still, I had no idea who this guy was, so I didn't get excited.

Then as we all started eating, the guys joked and laughed about earlier incidents. I heard them calling him Suge and Boss at the table. Yet, it still didn't register in my head that he was Suge Knight, Death Row CEO. I kept whispering to Casey every chance I got. I asked her if this guy was Suge because I kept hearing the guy across the table calling him Boss, but she didn't know herself.

I thought Suge Knight was loud and scary to be around, the way TV portrayed him to be, but this guy was quiet. So I asked one of the guys, and he said it was Suge Knight, the owner of Death Row Records like, if you don't know, you better ask somebody.

I wasn't interested before because I wasn't into light-skinned men. After I had assurance that he was, I got real interested. It was still hard for me to believe he was Suge Knight because TV made him look huge. He asked me to sit next to him and started asking me questions about my life. I pretended to be a little helpless with finances and everything. I even told him I didn't have a car to get around.

Suge took Casey and I back to his place, this big house in Beverly Hills, with a maid and butler. Tupac stayed there with us that night, and so did Suge. Casey said she wanted to have sex with Tupac. I felt she was a grown woman who could do as she wanted. I know I was. Tupac smiled the whole night. He had the smile of an angel. He was real comical though, and I loved it.

Suge's room was at the opposite end of Tupac's room. We all sat in Suge's room and talked for a while. On the floor was a case of Dom Pérignon champagne inside of a box. Casey and I sat on Suge's bed and waited, while he and Tupac left out of the room for about an hour. Where they went to, we have no idea.

Casey said she was going to screw Tupac and get inside of his head to find out about his life. She said she had a way to make people open up, and I told her, "Good luck with that one."

Finally, Tupac and Suge came back to the room, and Suge said he was tired.

Casey asked Tupac what he was about to do, and he said, "Chill." She asked if she could chill with him, and he told her to come on.

I stayed in the room with Suge. We talked about

his life a little bit, and about his plans, and he told me the whole story of how he came upon Tupac. I gave him a back rub and sat on his back. He had big shoulders and a big tattoo of a kid on his arms. I asked him if it was his baby picture, and he said it was a picture of his son. I wanted to know if he ever played football too, with those big legs and wide back. He said he did play football back in college in Miami.

I guess he was tired of all the questions, so he flipped over and asked me why I didn't have a man taking care of me.

Next thing I knew, we were screwing. I can't tell you to this day how Suge and I ended up screwing around. I just know we did. I was too high on drinks to remember everything, but I do remember using a condom with him that night.

I remember being a JUMPOFF to everybody else, but I simply do not remember how we got into sex that night.   I   do   remember   this—
It wasn't pleasing to the eye what I, well, Suge was

working with. Now that part of the night I do remember. I was disappointed, as if this big man knows he should be working with more than that.

I remember me getting on top of him. I was slim at the time, so he was too big to be on top of me.

Suge wasn't a small guy, but after seeing R. Kelly's monster hung down, I was spoiled. The only reason I didn't mind being his JUMPOFF was because I knew he would take care of me and give me all I needed. He liked beautiful women who gave him attention. After all, which red-blooded male doesn't?

When the sex was over with, I was glad and I fell asleep. He fell asleep and snored like a bull. I recall hitting him a few times because I couldn't sleep.

The next morning he was up before I was. I heard a maid talking in the hallway. Then I heard Suge ask her to clean the room after I got up. I also smelled food downstairs cooking, so I got up.

Suge came into the room and told me where to find the towels and an extra toothbrush. Then he said to get dressed and come downstairs for breakfast.

I loved the size of that house and the design. I was excited about being in a big mansion. After I got dressed, I asked him which room Casey was in, and he told me she was in Pac's room.

I went into Tupac's room and found Casey in the bathroom doing her hair. We talked about our night with the guys, and she told me Tupac was the bomb in bed. He wanted her to suck on his ballpark, which is what she called it at the time. But she declined to suck it because she was saving that for her husband. Then she said he got upset with her because she was asking him too many question about his life and his family.

She said she even asked him why he had the words "Thug Life" engraved in his stomach. She said it looked gay, and Tupac got offended.

He went all into his mother's life, saying she was on drugs at one point in her life. Tupac showed Casey the areas on his body where bullets went in. He still had two left in his body. One bullet was still in his upper shoulder and another one someplace else.

Casey wanted to feel his wounds. You have to be crazy to ask someone how it feels to be the target of bullets, but Casey did. I asked her how he felt about her asking him all those questions about his personal life, and she said he didn't like it and he told her, "Some things you don't need to know."

She said Tupac told her that she asked too many questions. He also told her she was pretty and needed to learn how to keep her mouth shut.

I was sitting on the counter, and Casey had her bra on doing her hair when Tupac walked back in the room to get his shirt. He looked at me and said my girl was a lot to deal with, that she wanted to know all about him and his family.

He said he didn't mind telling her some things about himself, but then she wanted to know everything about his mother and his father. She even wanted to know how his father died, and if he ever met him.

Tupac said he wasn't going to deal with that because even after he told her to stop asking so many questions, she still went on and on about his life, and he thought it was disrespectful of her.

Then Casey looked at him and said, "I feel like you didn't get enough love growing up. You're not a mean guy, so stop acting like you all hard." Then she went at him some more. "Just like that, thug life on your stomach. How are you going to be when you become an old man with a tattoo that says thug life?"

He said Casey was crazy and he didn't know how he ended up with her. He also said she better be glad she was pretty with perky tits. Then he asked me if she was always hard to deal with. To me she was no different from when I'd first met her.

Casey grabbed Tupac's hands and told him, "One week with you, and I will make you open up about your entire life to me."

Tupac said he didn't need a week with her and made himself real clear again that the only thing he liked on her was her breasts because they were prettier than most girls' he had seen.

Casey asked him if he was going to shower, and he told her no, he didn't stink.

She said, "You still need to wash your butt before you put a clean shirt on."

Then Tupac left and went downstairs. Casey was going on and on about how nasty it was of him to put on a clean shirt and not wash up.

I couldn't believe she asked him how many girls he'd slept with in his life. I laughed at her because she was funny. I asked her to hurry up so we could eat.

We went downstairs to eat and sat at the breakfast table with about 10 people, including Suge. I knew who Richie Rich was, but besides Suge and Tupac, I didn't know the other guys at the table.

While we were eating breakfast, Tupac and some other guy were rolling up a big fat blunt and passing it around the table. Casey asked the guy if she could have some, and Tupac shouted across the table at her,

"No!"

I guess she thought he was joking, so she asked him again if she could have some, and he said no again.

She got up from the table and went to the other side where Tupac was sitting and told him, "Stop playing and pass the weed."

His whole demeanor changed. He shouted out, "Bitch, stop begging! If it ain't offered to you, stop begging. I can't stand a begger. If you want some weed, go get yo' own shit!"

I don't know which nerve Casey struck, but she hit the right one. My eyebrows went up. He was just smiling with her upstairs now moments later, he was cursing her out. Meanwhile Suge sat at the end of the table with a giant cigar in his mouth.

Casey laughed. "Who you calling a bitch?"

Tupac said, "You. You're the only one begging for weed. You want some, get yo' own."

Casey, smiling the whole time, said she wasn't gonna trip because he was being ignorant, and that the word *bitch* didn't mean anything to her.

I thought for sure Suge was going to put us out, but I guess he let Tupac handle it himself.

Tupac looked at me and said, "Your girl needs to chill out."

I didn't say anything. I mean, I really didn't know what to say.

Casey asked Tupac what was he throwing a fit about. Then she said, "Only dogs throw fits."

Then she told Tupac that he sounded ghetto in front of everybody at the table. Tupac tried to ignore her by talking to the other guys.

Casey sat back down, but she was still needling him, going on and on. Tupac asked me to get my girl because he was getting a little tired of her mouth.

I got up from the table and asked Casey to come with me. At first she didn't want to, but then she got up and came anyway.

After breakfast, Tupac came into the den where I was watching TV, and we watched the video channel together.

I asked him why he did Casey like that at the table. He said because his homeboys were there, and it's not ladylike for her to ask for anything to smoke, especially from another guy.

Then he said, "A lady shouldn't get high in front of everybody. She should do it in private if she's gon' smoke. She could have told me upstairs she wanted some weed, not while the niggas doing it." Then he added, "She didn't know what could have been rolled up in that weed." He thought Casey was out of place and very disrespectful to him.

All I know is, they had known each other a day, and they were at it like they had known each other for years.

10

DATING SUGE KNIGHT; THE DRAMA CONTINUES

I ran into Suge going up the stairs, and he gave me some money to buy clothes for Casey and myself. He'd also arranged for his assistant to pick us up that afternoon.

What surprised me the most was when Suge told me that I need to slap my girl because she was way out of line. I was confused. No one had ever told me to slap my girl for talking too much. I wasn't into slapping folks, especially my girl, no matter what she did. Casey was a grown woman. What would I look like slapping her? I couldn't tell her what to do.

Suge insisted that if Casey got out of line again, that I would need to slap her.

I went upstairs to talk to Casey. I let her know that Suge wanted me to slap her, and she laughed her ass off.

Everything was always funny to Casey. She wasn't hip at all to the streets, but she wanted to hang around thugs. She said her ex-boyfriend was a thug, that she had been through a lot with him.

Suge and Tupac left, and later on that day, one of Suge's assistants came to pick us up in a van and took us to the hotel to check in. As well as staying at the house, Casey and I shared a room at the Marriot Hotel under Death Row's account. After we checked

125

our things into the hotel, we rode over to the studio to meet Suge and Tupac.

A guy named Six Nine (who married Vivica Fox a few years later) took us over to the studio in a minivan. He was part of the male group, Six Feet Deep, from Atlanta. He was very tall, with an ugly blonde dye in his hair. He was interested in Casey, and the other singer, Six Eight was interested in me. Neither of them knew I was Suge's JUMPOFF at the time. It was nobody's business.

By the time we arrived at the studio, Tupac and Suge were standing outside waiting for us. The security at the studio was real tight. They never searched Suge, but they searched everybody else who came through, including Tupac. You could not even enter the studio unless you were willing to let the security scan your whole body. And if you had any weapons on you, security would hold it for you. Before Tupac was scanned, I remember him handing his gun to security.

It was a little scary at first. The studios in Chicago weren't that extreme where security guards had weapons and you had to go through a scanner before entering.

We went straight into the studio room and sat in on Tupac's session with Richie Rich. This is where we met Rage the rapper, who stood tall with brown freckles. She was nice. I thought she was going to be mean, but she was totally the opposite. She was actually one of the nicest people I'd met in a long time. She was almost like the soft candy. Well, maybe until you pissed her off or something. Her natural voice was much softer than her rapping voice.

We talked for a while. She told me she stayed to herself, that the guys there were jealous of her because they all started living at the hotel, but after a year, Suge moved her into an apartment because she was tired of staying in the house the Outlawz were staying at. She was the only female rapper on the label at the time.

Kurupt and Casey hit it off pretty well after Casey found out he had a pocketful of weed to smoke. He asked Casey to go outside and smoke with

127

him.

I stayed inside, sat behind Tupac, and listened in on his session. We had a good conversation about the music business. He was telling me how easy it was for him to write about all the wickedness. He thought I was cool to hang out with. I realized he was smarter and more intelligent than people thought he was. He said, while he was locked up, a lot of truths just came to him out of nowhere.

Tupac sat next to the engineer going over his lyrics, while Richie Rich was in the booth dropping a verse.

Earlier Six Nine had said Suge had a woman, and it was known that he beat on his women. I was sure Suge did have a woman. He had too much money to be single. I wasn't his woman, I was his JUMPOFF and I didn't care. I knew what I wanted from him, and he knew what he wanted from me.

Later that night, we all went back to the house. Tupac and Casey ended up together, and Suge and I ended up having a few drinks. I was beginning to like

Suge a little bit more. No matter how bossy he was, I knew I could still get what I wanted from him. Although I had a thing for dark guys and Suge was light-skinned, I still kicked it with him because he had something to offer a girl. So I would drink his champagne, get tipsy, and have sex with him.

The reason I don't remember much of our sex experiences was because it was quick, and more like a "Wham! Bam! Thank you, executive of the record label." There was nothing exciting about my sex life with Suge. He was decent, but do I get wet from reminiscing? No.

Shortly, Casey and I was picked up by a driver, who then took us to the hotel. Six Feet Deep was in the lobby, and a few of them came to our room to hang out and smoke some weed. We all had a few drinks and talked about where we were all from.

The guys started coming on to us, but we had no interest in them at all.

Tyrone, ghostwriter for Death Row Records, came into our room and smoked with Casey. I tried smoking some and choked on it. Casey said I wasn't smoking it right.

Tyrone was hanging with us because he would be our writer, and he hung with us most of that afternoon. Then we all went to the studio together.

As soon as I made it to the studio, Suge called me into his office and closed the door. It was my first time going into his office with his Death Row red-and-white rug on the floor. He asked me not to step on the rug, so I walked around it and sat on the desk.

He started questioning me about our ride and the male singing group. He wanted to know what happened at the hotel. I told him that we just hung out with the guys.

Then he said, "I am with you, which means you will not date anyone else. You got it?"

That was fine by me, since I had no interest in anyone else.

He touched my arms and said I needed to go shopping for a new wardrobe. He didn't like the way I dressed. He thought I looked too soft and dressed too sexy. He said I was turning the guys on, that from now on when I come to the studio, I needed to wear bigger pants and put on a baseball cap, to look harder to represent Death Row.

That was the start of his craziness right then. Suge took his cap off his head, put it on my head, and said it looked nice, and that is how I should be. He told me to keep the cap on so I could get comfortable with it.

Suge hit a nerve because I wasn't used to a man telling me what to do, how to do it, and when to do it. But that day, I chose to keep the baseball cap on.

As I was leaving out, he asked me to tell the boys to come back in. On my way out of his office, I grabbed a bottle of Dom Pérignon champagne. I looked at the 10 different surveillance monitors and thought, *Wow!*

131

Casey was in the kitchen area. When she found out Suge had me wearing a baseball cap, she said, "Oh, he's trying to control you."

We realized there was no privacy in the studio. The only safe area to do anything was in the bathroom. So we would go in the restroom whenever we wanted to talk.

Casey said I should be careful with Suge because of the things Kurupt had told her, things I shouldn't repeat.

That same night we went inside of Studio Room A, where Tupac had a session going on. We sat in on his session and watched him record his song.

KC from Jodeci came in and started chatting with us. I had to compliment the brother on his vocals because I loved to hear him sing. We all sat over to the side so we wouldn't disturb Tupac, who seemed to be concentrating real hard that day.

DJ Quick was in the other room finishing up the song, "How Do You Want It," which was the reason

KC was there that night. KC was sloppy drunk that night. When I looked at him real good, all I thought about was how TV makes you look better, because he reminded me of *Gremlins*.

KC had his drink in his hand, trying to rap to Casey. Then he said to me, "I bet you Suge's girl, huh. You look like his type."

Casey, who was high too, asked him what Suge's type is, and KC replied, "Your girl right there!"

Meanwhile, Tupac was in the booth at the time all of this was going on.

Napoleon from the Outlawz came inside and instantly got into the conversation with Casey and KC. I couldn't hear the whole conversation because I was paying attention to Tupac in the booth.

All I heard was Napoleon say to Casey, "Oh, you one of those girls who's stuck-up."

By that time, Tupac came out of the recording

booth and sat next to the engineer, as if he was totally ignoring the conversation.

KC picked up a pen and started writing, and Tupac told him, if he was going to write, he had to leave because he didn't want folks "biting" his lyrics. KC politely left out, and I was thinking, *Wasn't he just on the song with Pac?* It all seemed a little weird to me.

Napoleon and Casey were still griping, and I could tell Tupac was getting antsy. His focus was on us then.

Napoleon was drunk, and I heard him say he couldn't stand pretty girls, that he would pour some liquor on her hair from the bottle he had in his hands. Casey said she would whip his ass if he poured liquor on her hair.

Tupac got real upset. He was more upset that day than he was at the breakfast table with Casey. All of a sudden he stopped writing, jumped up from his chair, and told her to get out because she wasn't going to whip no nigga's ass. Then he said, "A bitch is a bitch, and a nigga is a nigga, and you need to stay in a bitch place." Then he told her to get out, so I left out too.

For some reason Tupac didn't like the fact that she was in the studio in his session talking to other guys. It wasn't all about what Casey had said to Napoleon, but more that Tupac had gotten jealous she was talking to the guys in his session.

When Tupac came out the studio, I asked him why did he say that to Casey.

He said, "I'm tired of Casey running her mouth, knowing she can't whip my niggas. She needs to learn how to handle herself." Then he added, "I didn't mean any harm to you, but these my niggas, they expect me to be a certain way. I can't let them see anything other than me being me."

I knew then that Tupac had a soft heart underneath when we stood outside that studio and talked. No matter what he said, I told him it wasn't necessary for him to go off on Casey like that because his boy disrespected her first by saying he was going to pour some liquor in her hair.

"That's why I put them out, too. I didn't invite them or nobody in my session anyway. Niggas come in my session tryin'-a bite my lyrics. If I catch a nigga tryin'-a bite my lyrics, we gon' have beef."

He went from one subject to another one, and I knew then that he was disturbed that day, or just couldn't concentrate. He said deep down inside he wasn't a hard guy, but around his boys, he couldn't be all soft. He also said he had an image to portray, and that he really didn't mean to go that far with her.

Tupac liked me and thought I was cool, but he felt like Casey needed to learn how to act. He had a problem with her going around there and smoking with the guys. He felt it was disrespectful to him. Then he said he was through with her, that she was crazy.

Tupac said he was trying to get through with his music there because he was getting tired of all the things he had to put up with, and of the guys and how they acted.

I didn't know where all of that was coming from, but he said those words to me. He seemed unhappy that night, like something else was going on.

People started coming around us, so he stopped talking to me and went back inside his session to finish up.

I knew I could go back inside his session, but I didn't, since he didn't want Casey in there.   As usual, Casey couldn't understand why he was so angry with her.

I told her, "He thinks you're crazy."

But she thought he was crazy too because, as she told it, one minute, when they're in bed he wants to change then the next minute he wants to act all hard. However, I told her we needed to concentrate on us and not get caught up in all this other stuff.

Kevin, Suge's assistant, wanted to talk to us about getting on the schedule next month to work with DJ Quick, but Casey didn't want to deal with

Death Row anymore. It didn't matter to me either, but I wanted to go to Death Row's Christmas party, since everyone was saying that Death Row threw the best parties.

11

NIGHTMARE ON SUGE KNIGHT STREET

The next day I woke up from a dream and told Casey about it. In my dream Suge was trying to kill me. Then I saw a girl in my dream I had never met. She had black eyes from Suge beating her up. Casey thought that might be a bad omen, since he did tell me to slap her.

We met up with Tyrone later that day at the studio, and Danny Boy, who was from Chicago too, came in the break room joking with us. We started talking about people we knew back home.

I was still seeing Suge. Yeah, I was his JUMPOFF, but I never knew where his main house was. Of course, the house we stayed at with Tupac wasn't his main house. He did what he was supposed to do, so I didn't complain. I just didn't like having to go to his accountant whenever I wanted something; only because I had to wait on Suge's accountant to contact him to get approval before getting what I asked for.

I started to feel like I was a trick after a while because I was used to getting what I want; straight from the source. Usually I would stay in a situation to get what I want, but I wasn't in control of this situation, and that was different for me.

Next time we went to the studio, Tupac was there in the waiting room relaxing on his back with a female at the time, with his head on her lap. They looked mad at each other.

I gave Casey the eye, like there is your man girl. He's got a new chick.

I went in Suge's office to have a talk with him. I told him I was ready to go home. He said I needed to stay because he had projects coming up for film, that he knew I wanted to do some acting also, and he would make sure I had a role.

He also reminded me of Death Row's Christmas party that was going on in a few days, which was going to be held at his other house in Laurel Canyon in Hollywood Hills.

Casey and I showed up at Death Row's Christmas party. Inside of the house was nice and white with a big-screen TV showing porn. Dr. Dre was there looking real sexy, as well as a few other well-known celebs.

When Suge arrived there with Tupac, the cameras were all over them. The media was interviewing Tupac as he made his way through the crowd.

Once the attention died down, I walked up to Tupac and hugged him. I also talked to Suge and told him I wanted to go home for the holidays, and he told me to let Ron know, and he would book the flight for me. I asked him if he could let Ron know, so I wouldn't have to wait for Ron to contact him before he did it.

The party was jumping that night. They were right about Death Row parties.

I had a lot of things running through my head that night. I was drinking a lot and mixing my drinks with light and dark liquor. Before long I was toasted.

I went up to Dr. Dre to let him know how sexy he was, and that I would love a chance to get at him. He smiled and asked me if I was okay.

Casey grabbed me and said his girlfriend was on the other side of the bar. She also told me it wasn't wise to talk to Dre at the party because someone would tell Suge, and if he found out I was flirting with

Dre, it would be trouble. She'd grabbed me too soon because I wanted to get his number.

Casey said I was acting like a whore. I told her, "Whores are sexy, and sluts are even sexier."

She knew I was drunk then because my words were slurred. I know I pissed her off bad that night. I don't know what got into me because I had no control of myself.

She took me upstairs on the balcony where a few people were, so I could sit down and sober up. Well, she left me alone up there, and I started throwing up. She saw me throwing up from downstairs. Talk about embarrassing Casey. She couldn't even have a good time because she felt responsible for me.

All I remember was one of the guys carrying me to the van to take me to the hotel. The whole time Casey talked about me and how angry she was at me for getting drunk.

She stood by me though. She didn't let me make

a fool of myself.

I felt bad because I knew I was too sexy for something like that to happen.

The next morning when I woke up, Casey said I threw up and fell asleep in the chair and she didn't want anyone to see me like that. My body felt like crap, and I had a hangover. I stayed in the hotel the whole day.

I told her I felt evil spirits at that house, and she said she had been saying that all along but I wasn't listening to her.

But that wasn't it. I just thought she was crazy half of the time, especially when she started talking about her psychic instincts.

She laughed at me and started playing around with some silver psychic balls the size of a golf ball. She also suggested that I should try meditation because it helped her to understand people, but I didn't want her to think I believed some silver balls gave her psychic power. She also said that she wanted to go ahead and stay with Death Row Records, but thought I should stop messing with Suge.

We both knew that wasn't gonna happen. It was too late. The bottom line was, I'd had enough, and was ready to go back home to Chicago. She said once I left, she was going to leave too.

Monday, we were back in the studio writing with Tyrone. The lyrics he had given us were crazy and too hard. He wanted us to talk about pulling triggers, something I knew nothing about. I was trying to get that through Tyrone's head. I mean, really, how do I go from being a reigning beauty queen, to pulling triggers? I'd never pulled a trigger in my life, though if I had to, I would.

He said, "Hey, Rage ain't never pulled a trigger either, but she raps as if she has."

The bottom line was, he had to give us lyrics we could relate to, like getting money or something, not blasting somebody and putting them in the trunk of a car. I was too much of a lady to walk around talking like a gangster.

He tried to convince us that Suge would have us rapping no other way but hard.

Casey was uncomfortable with it, and so was I. So we decided we couldn't rap his hardcore lyrics. People wouldn't accept two girls rapping hard, if they didn't look the part. Rage could do it because it fit her.

Later on that day, Suge came to the studio and called me to the back room. He'd heard we had a problem with Tyrone's lyrics. It didn't feel real, and I would be a fake to pretend that I was hard when I wasn't. My style wasn't to piss people off over lyrics. I didn't want to be that type of rapper that had to watch every move I made.

Suge thought it was a good image to have because Death Row artists represented the rough side.

Well, no one had said that in the beginning. I couldn't get through to him, so I changed the subject and asked him for a bottle of champagne.

We were interrupted by the rap artist Kurupt when he came in and asked Suge a question, so I left out to find Casey, who was outside smoking as usual.

We saw Six Nine outside in the minivan and caught a ride back to the hotel with him. He was a little uneasy about the label because his group had been there for over a year and Suge hadn't put a single out on them. Six Nine was so frustrated, he said he was leaving the group and going back home to Atlanta because they were not in a good situation. He was complaining the whole time about Suge and everyone else involved in the label.

I was surprised to hear out of 2 years, they were only receiving two hundred and fifty dollars. He had asked me not to say anything to Suge, but in the same breath, he was saying he wasn't afraid of him.

When we made it back to our room, I told Casey I was ready to move on. I would rather keep pursuing acting, instead of dealing with all the drama Death Row had to offer.

The next morning, Casey and I packed our bags up. Then we called Tyrone and told him we were leaving to go home. We told him how we felt about everything, and he understood.

Because he shared a room with two other people, he asked if he could have our room, since Suge booked it for a month at a time. We had no problem with that.

Casey drove to the studio, but no one was there working that day. It was early, and producers didn't come in until the afternoon. I wrote Suge a nice, nasty note and slid it underneath his office door. Yes, he was looking for me, but I was already on my way back to Chicago.

Back at home in Chicago, it was a while before my sister knew about me seeing Suge.

I did talk to Tupac again and let him say hi to my sister, who loved him. Sad to say, it was the last time I spoke to Tupac before he was shot and killed.

I remember Casey called me and asked me if I had heard he was shot while with Suge in Vegas. I could not believe it.

12

GETTING DIRTY IN ATLANTA

I lost contact with a lot of my L.A. friends, besides Casey. I got back into a singing group with Oobie and Dee, who was a friend of mine and Oobie's at the time.

Dee used to sleep around with my next-door neighbor back home in Chicago. She'd moved down to Atlanta and started dancing as a stripper at this club called Nicky's. She would call us all the time and ask us when and if we would come to Atlanta.

I convinced Oobie we should go, since Dee talked about how nice it was and how much money she was making getting naked every night. We went to Atlanta to see Dee, and when we got down there, we barely recognized her because she had lost so much weight. I thought she was on drugs or something.

I remember she came home from work early one day because one of the girls had stolen her money. She had been at work for 5 hours. When we found out that she'd only made 35 dollars within those 5 hours, I told her she needed to quit stripping there, because she wasn't making money.

The next day we went down to G's Place. Dee told us that the rapper Too Short had a studio inside of this rim shop, so we went down there to see. As soon as we walked through the door, G was at the counter and asked us if we were a singing group, and we said yes. At the time, the name of the group was SML, which stand for small, medium, and large. We met Too Short, and instantly he liked us and put us in the studio.

Dee started talking to every producer we ran into. She wanted to sleep with Too Short, but he didn't want her. He actually wanted me, but I never found him attractive. The shit he talked about turned me on more than anything.

About a week later, Dee got an attitude with Oobie over who would sing lead. My voice wasn't strong enough to sing lead, and Oobie had the prettier voice of the two of us.

A few days later, we were in the studio recording a couple of songs, and Dee started to get a little ridiculous. She was out of control with her attitude and stormed out of the studio. When we made it back to her apartment, she was real silent with me and Oobie.

She would catch an attitude with her brother, who she thought was taking our side against her, but he was only being honest about her ways.

The next morning, Dee still had the same

attitude, mainly with Oobie, because she was the lead singer in the group. So Oobie asked her to stop being a bitch and come on with it.

Dee got offended and was ready for us to leave her apartment because she hadn't made any money and was tired of going to the studio to not get a chance to sing a song she wrote. But that call was on J Mac, our producer at the time, who made the decision on who would sing lead. They got into a heated argument, so Dee put me, Oobie, her brother and her so-called boyfriend out. She called the police on us, and they came to the house and said we had to go because she wanted us out.

Her brother drove us to get something to eat. While we were sitting down to eat, I got up to use the restroom, and Dee's boyfriend came into the bathroom behind me while I was fixing my pants back together. I was stunned.

He asked me if he could lick my kitty. I was so upset with Dee, I let him, and right in the bathroom.

Dee was scandalous to us, so I figured…Why not let her dog-ass man lick, lick, lick away? I really didn't care at the time because she knew we had nowhere to go, and she went as low as to put us out of her place and call the police on us. A friend wouldn't do that. That wasn't a friend to do something like that, all because her voice wasn't prettier than Oobie's.

So as we all got back in the car after leaving the eatery, I let Dee's boyfriend continue where he left off at in the bathroom. He got me real hot, and I screwed him. Oobie was sitting on the front passenger seat, and Dee's brother was doing the driving. I tuned them both out, and went on with the program.

We finally made it to Dee's boyfriend's place to drop him off. He lived on the east side of Atlanta, off Ponce de Leon. He wanted me to think he was done messing with Dee and thought he had a chance of seeing me again, but he had nothing coming. I used him because he came on to me, and to show Dee that her man she'd been screwing and claiming to be her number one piece was actually a piece of garbage.

After Dee's brother dropped us off at the hotel, we called up Too Short and told him what happened.

The next day we went to the studio and met with Short   and   G. G just couldn't understand what it was about female groups, and why they are never long-lasting. He thought it was foul for Dee to throw us out the way she did. He informed me he had talked to her just before we'd arrived, and that she was torn over my sleeping with her boyfriend.

To my understanding, he was no longer her boyfriend, and I didn't want the trick anyways. G thought it was weak for Dee to gripe over boyfriend stuff, saying it was nothing.

Men come a dime a dozen, and he wasn't paying her bill's, so he was like spilled milk anyway. At the end of the day, Dee really was jealous of Oobie and wanted to sing lead on songs.

G said to me, "If you can't handle the small things,

then you surely cannot handle the entertainment business. Don't ever cry over a boy in the industry."

The truth of the matter was, Dee had slept with J Mac. Then she got pissed because she was a JUMPOFF, and he let Oobie sing lead.

So we stayed away from the studio for about a week, and Oobie started seeing her friend Emanuel, a songwriter and producer for Mariah Carey at the time. They liked each other a lot. He was good to Oobie, buying her all types of expensive jewelry.

One night Oobie was gone with Emanuel, and I got bored. So I called up a guy named Robert, whom I'd met a while ago, giving us directions. Robert starred in a reality show called *Amateur Millionaires Club*. We hit it off, and the sex was good.

One day I invited him to the studio in a recording session and Too Short didn't like it. Short pulled me to the side to tell me that he usually didn't let in strangers. But Robert was no stranger, he was my guest. I thought it was strange for Short to say that to me.

After we were done recording, Short called me on the phone and said I need to be "married to the family" before I started bringing outside people in. I had no idea what he was talking about. He thought I was trying to be funny, but I wasn't. I didn't know what married to the family meant.

Then Murder Dog, one of Too Short's friends, said it meant I needed to screw somebody in the camp. Nobody in the camp had smacked my booty. If that's all it was, Short should have said so. I would have let him smack me on the booty all the time. He was so busy talking about strippers and big tits around me, and I wasn't a stripper, so he didn't pursue me enough.

A few days later, we were in a recording session again, and Short said I throw curve balls at him.

After the session, he wanted Oobie and I to go out with him, and I already had plans with Robert. So he got mad at me and made little comments to me, like, "Oh, you gon' get wit' cho baby daddy, huh."

I ignored it most of the time. I knew he didn't like that I was seeing Robert. After a while, Short and I didn't get along well. And I didn't like J Mac. His head was too big. I had already gone through this controlling thing with Suge, so I wasn't about to do it again.

I decided to stop working with Short Records, and I explained my reason to Oobie. She respected my decision and stayed with them for a little while longer.

It was a few years later when I ran into Too Short, and he asked me why I never gave him no booty. He should have said he wanted the booty. So we met up one night at his house, and he was my JUMPOFF. Short was pleasing that night.

If I had any idea he was that nice, I would have screwed him as much as I could a lot sooner. There were many nights I needed company for the moment. He was sexy with it too. We were supposed to get in his hot tub, but we never made it there to it.

I enjoyed that moment with him. But my thing is,

the sex has to be over the moon to make me want more from you. It was nice, but it didn't reach the moon. But, given a chance, would I screw him again? No. I had it already. Not that he wasn't good, but I had that.

13

MR. FLAMBOYANT CAKE AND ICE CREAM, ROBERT JACKSON

I loved me some Robert Jackson... in the beginning. You're talking dark and handsome and eating my kitty while I was on my menstrual. That was different.

My girlfriend Ladee Storm said, "Jara, you let that man get a taste of blood, honey, he would be hard to get rid of," and she ain't never lied.

Robert was my sweetheart though. I was his Bonnie, his ride-or-die chick, and he was my Clyde. At least that's what my brother-in-law called us, which I had no problem with.

Robert was good to me. He was a hustler, stayed on his grind, and always had the finer things in life because he had to impress his hoes, and that's how he kept the ladies coming. Then again, I pretty much had that sewn up. The more I took from him, the less he had for lurkers.

Robert was so smooth with his outside women, he would tell them I was his baby momma, that I needed a place to stay, and he could not leave me out on the streets. Everything about that was a lie. That is the most tired excuse I have ever heard, but women fell for his lies, though.

The thing with me was, If I didn't see him do it, then I had no proof, so he wasn't guilty of anything.

He was a ladies' man, and he was fine. I will give him that much.

Now the positive things were, he was supportive of my career, he helped me in many situations, and he hired a producer, who is still a friend, to record a full album on me. Truth is, Robert built a studio and formed an independent record label just for me.

My issue with him, was he was way too out there in the streets, but when it came to me doing my thing, there was a problem. Typical man crap—Always want their cake with ice cream.

Another issue I had, was we fought sometimes. There were two sides to him, nice guy and the devil. I even have a permanent scar on my face from us fighting. Our fight could come from my being too flip. The ghetto in me came out sometimes, and many nights I threw beer bottles at him. It might seem funny now, but it wasn't so funny at the time. Any relationship that has violence is dangerous, but I wasn't one of those weak chicks to let a man kick my butt.

Like many relationships, in the beginning it's good. Then as time went by, I wondered if I was in the right situation. I knew it wasn't the right one for me. I need space in a relationship, just like most men do.

Robert had to know when I was going and coming, checking up on my every move. Not cool at all. We would have problems if I didn't answer my phone when he called.

At any rate, I got to know and become friends with his sister Rakia. She and I would hang tight. She knew her brother. She never wanted to get involved, and I didn't want her to either, but she was cool.

After a while, I saw no change in Robert. I was getting tired of the relationship, and I wanted more. I was becoming more mature and realized there was more to life than cars and material things, which was what Robert was all about.

As long as I had a luxury bank account, you can have all of that other stuff. I didn't like to show off. He even tried to dress me sometimes, and we had totally different tastes. His taste was more like, the shoes has to match the shirt. Not that I didn't like the look, but I just didn't like it for him because sometimes the color would put me in the mind of clown wear.

My relationship with Robert had started to get boring, so the next thing up was to bring him another woman, since he was a cheater anyway, and that is what he liked so much. I had gotten to the point that I did not mind him sleeping with other women just as long as he was giving me what I needed.

Toward the end of relationship, I brought a total of three of my friends to screw him, and they did. I was there, and I watched. Then that wasn't happening anymore. In the beginning, it was fun to be in bed with him while he would screw other women, it turned me on, made me hot, but after a while, it got boring.

The relationship had turned sour, and I knew he wasn't the man I would marry one day because he was dangerously loose. I had no more trust in him.

It's one thing to be a JUMPOFF, but to screw your JUMPOFF with no condom…really?

That is why these celebs and important people get in trouble today with their JUMPOFFS. They go out and have sex with the JUMPOFF. Then when the JUMPOFF gets pregnant, they want to cry about it. Strap up.

If Robert had not gotten into a little Fed trouble, I don't know what would have become of that relationship. But when he left to do some time in prison, my life took another turn.

Even as a married man, he still would come on to me. But I have yet to have sex with him since our breakup. Not that I am doing his very unattractive lady—I think she is a lady—a favor by not being his JUMPOFF, I just don't want him in that way. We're friends.

14

THE SEX, THE DRUGS, THE TRICKS, AND SHAQ

I went to visit my cousin in Los Angeles, and what was supposed to have been a visit turned into a 6-month stay. He had a friend named Renee that he stayed with. She was sweet, petite, sexy, and wild. Sometimes she worked as a call girl. Her good friend was a known celebrity madam who knew how to have fun too.

After I was there a few days, Renee asked her friend if I could come along with them sometimes on her calls. The madam didn't mind. She knew I was in town for a short while to pursue a career in acting.

The first call I ever went on with Renee was when she had to meet with Shaq. Renee didn't mind servicing his needs because he would kick her down real sweet with extra money. You would think she would be all over Shaq because he played in the NBA. What groupie wouldn't try to trap him down?

I do not know how many times she saw him altogether, but I know within the time I stayed with her, it was at least three times. I know he liked her because the madam had other girls to offer him, but that's not who he wanted. He wanted Renee.

There would be a lot of times I would go and meet up with Renee and her madam friend just before I went in for bed.

The madam always would be at the hottest

parties in Hollywood. She was on her money. She serviced a lot of people. People you would never have thought would want a girl because they seemed to have the perfect little life in the public eye with their wife.

My lifestyle at this point was a whole lot faster than the days I'd experienced with Death Row.

I actually liked the madam as a person, and would often hang out with her. One day she asked me if I wanted to go to a party in Hollywood Hills. I thought it might be good for me to meet some people in the entertainment business. I met the madam at her house and jumped in her jeep with her. The whole time, she was on the phone, making sure her girls were all together and ready to make money that night.

We arrived at this beautiful mansion, which was way greater than Suge's house. I walked into the mansion with the madam. The lights in the house were dimmed. I followed the madam upstairs, and she introduced me to some white Hollywood film producers. Then she told me to help myself to whatever.

I saw food, but I wasn't hungry. So I was admiring the house and the artwork on the walls. I had seen expensive paintings in my lifetime, but the paintings they had on the walls were ridiculous. They included paintings by Edvard Munch and Pablo Picasso. I called up a friend of mine and asked her if she had heard of the painters because I wasn't the only one admiring the artwork. She said those painters were out of her league.

The madam was upstairs, and I was downstairs and knew no one. A female came and sat next to me to talk. She wanted to know who was I there with. She seemed a little out of it. Then she asked me if I wanted to go upstairs and party. I was confused, because it was a party.

I told her we were at the party, but she was talking about going upstairs to get high. When I told her I didn't get high, she looked at me as if I was the crazy one and asked me why was I even there. She was too stoned for me to carry on a conversation with her. I told her who invited me, and that I thought it was going to be a different type of party.

She said that's why it is called a party. It's not a club party, it's a people party. I went upstairs with her anyway to find the madam and found her in the bedroom with four other people getting wasted. So much free powder was around that any and everybody could help themselves to it.

The madam looked at me and said she only did it sometimes, not all the time. She didn't have to explain to me what she did, she was a grown woman.

Then I saw her put this water up her nose, and I asked her what that was for. She explained to me that it kept her nose from burning so bad. I feel like I would be torturing myself to do something to make my nose burn.

The owner of the house, a friend she had known for a few years, came over and whispered something in her ear. As he whispered in her ear, she looked at me and started talking to him.

After he left out of the room, she offered me some powder that was on the plate. She asked me to try a little bit. I didn't want to party, and I told her my decision was firm.

I had been at this party for 2 hours, and everyone seemed spaced the hell out. I knew the streets, but this was a bunch of wealthy people at this party. At a ghetto party, you have to worry about fights and gunshots breaking out. But at a party with the wealthy, you have to worry about who is shoving powder up their nose, and make sure you don't drink from the wrong glass.

So before the night ended, the madam said that her friend who owned the place wanted to get with me. She said he thought I was attractive. She told him I was a friend, not a working girl. She also told me his wife was not there. She was at the house in New York, and hardly ever visited the L.A. property.

I shocked her when I told her I would do it. I said, "Honey, he can have this kitty as long as he pays well." Why not? I knew I would probably never see him again in life, so if he wanted to get with me, bring it on.

The madam told me I could get anything I wanted out of him because he was loaded with cash, that he was also known to be a big fat trick. That was all I needed to hear. I told her 10 stacks.

First of all, his wife had no idea he was tricking with a JUMPOFF. I was surely his JUMPOFF that night. When I know a man is married, if I decide to be his JUMPOFF for whatever reason, I will try my best to break him for every dollar he's got.

She looked at me and laughed because she had never charged that much for anyone. But it didn't matter if she did or not. I didn't work for her. She had all of these friends in these high places, so if they wanted a girl like me for sex then they had to pay.

What do I look like, being this filthy rich guy's JUMPOFF for one night, and he does nothing for me besides screw me? How hot is that? It's not. So I made his ass pay for it, and it wasn't peanut money either.

She smiled at me and continued to party, and before the night was over, I got exactly what I asked for. I had sex with this man upstairs in his bathroom on the floor. Where he got the cash from, I didn't care. I knew the money was real. Call it what you want, but I won't ever forget it.

I really thought he would say I was crazy for asking for that amount of money and say forget it.

So the next night came, and I was still tired from the night before. The madam said Renee had to be at a porno party, and she had a few other girls working there. I knew wherever she would be, celebs would be there, or some very powerful people. No matter how tired I was, I wanted to go.

I had never been to a porno party before, so I was surprised as hell when they charged 2 hundred dollars at the door. This porno party was inside of a suite at a hotel and it wasn't that big.

I saw two well-known black porn stars there. I met

John Singleton that night. He was shorter than I expected. He was at the party hanging out with the girls inside of the bedroom. I also met another actor with John, but I never knew his name, though I had seen him in quite a few black films before. And a few NBA players came on in too.

The party was sweet. The two porno girls put on a show that night. I was living it up, partying with a classy female pimp and a call girl. It was fun, but it wasn't my world. I realized, if I continued to hang out with Renee and this working madam, I would get caught up in their world.

I could have continued to go to these parties with her and been someone's JUMPOFF every time, or I could have worked for a female pimp and have my 15 minutes of fame. To me that wasn't success, and I didn't see any longevity. Besides, I don't do well with pimps. I have never been pimped, and I can't screw someone and give up my money to a pimp. Not ever happening. So I tried to get more involved with my acting career and went out less with them.

15

JAZZE PHA/BUTTERBALL TURKEY

One night I was in Atlanta, and I hooked back up with Robert's sister, Rakia. We went out that night, and that's when I met Jazze Pha. He came up to me as the club was closing and said he loved the colors in the top I wore and then he asked me my name and if he could have my number. I told him to give me his number, but I didn't have my purse with me that night. So he said to tell him the number and he would remember it. I shouted my phone number out to him over the music.

He remembered the number because he called me as soon as he got in the car, and we talked briefly.

That same night, Rakia and I went back to my place and ate some cheese eggs at three in the morning.

So the next day, Jazze called me, and I invited him to my place to pick me up. He came right over.

My cousin Ebony from the Midwest was there at the time he came over. When he made it over, I wasn't quite ready, so he waited in the family room, where my cousin was, while I finished curling my hair.

We left the house and went to grab a bite to eat. As we sat at the table, he ordered my food which was one entreé then he ordered his. I had never seen anybody order as much food at one time the way he did. No wonder he was so big. All his food went to his stomach.

While we waited for the meal to come, we started to talk about the music business. He told me about his father being from Alabama and in the music business, and a few other things. Then he told me he had an artist named Ciara on his label, Sho'nuff Records. He talked about how he had to talk to Ciara about sleeping around with a lot of guys.

We had a few drinks before the meal came, and I learned a lot about his family in Alabama in that short time.

His meal came, and he ate everything on his plate. I was in shock. All I could think about was, he had to spend a lot of money just to eat.

When we were done eating, he took me back home because I had other things to do. Plus, my cousin was there.

He wanted me to go to the studio with him and I told him, "Maybe later. A friend and my cousin will probably come with me to the studio."

We got back to my place, and he was fascinated with my house and the decoration.

I took him for a tour in my house and showed him around. When we got in my bedroom, he grabbed and hugged me and then tried to kiss me. I didn't like the way his breath smelled, so I turned my head. It was my first time being that close up on him, and as I hugged him around his neck, he didn't smell too clean.

But it was a hot day, and by him being big, I thought maybe he could have sweated and gotten too hot and that's why he didn't smell clean. So I didn't think too much of it.

I did tell him that a dinner doesn't make me drop my panties. Only if I wanted to get loose. He smiled and let go of me.

I walked him downstairs, gave him a bottle of water, told him to call me later, and let him out.

Later that night, he called, and I went down to

the studio while he was working on some things with Manny Fresh. I stayed for a bit, but I needed to go home to take my cousin to the airport early that next morning.

Jazze asked me why I had to leave so soon and if he could come over to my place later, and I told him no. No man comes over my house after hours. Off limits!

Later on during the week, we went out to an event. I had gotten tipsy, and afterward, he and I went to the hotel in Buckhead. We really just went to chill out there. He told me that he was too drunk to drive.

The whole time we were there, his friends were blowing up his cell phone, trying to get him to come out to the strip club. But he was too tired.

Then one of his people called him to listen to Ciara's song that they had just started playing in the club. He was excited to let me hear it over the loud speaker. I told him that his artist and his production sounded good. So we sat around and talked for a short while.

I watched him smoke a little something as he sat on the bed. He took his pants off, and all I could see was his stomach.

He ordered a bottle of wine for me and asked me if I was hungry, and I told him no.

When I was finished drinking the wine, I sat on the bed next to him and told him he was a big man. By now the wine was talking, not me. I told him that I love a big man and that a big man turns me on.

He looked at me and said I was real pretty. Then he asked me why I didn't have a boyfriend. I told him not to worry about all of that. So then he asked me what is it I was trying to do with him because I was rubbing his stomach. I told him I wanted to see what he was working with.

I asked him to take off his shorts, and he did. So when he took them off, I told him he wasn't so bad. He just had a big stomach. But he seemed a little embarrassed.

I took his underwear off and started looking for his dome, but I didn't see it. So I lifted his stomach up and pulled some of his skin back. "Oh, there it is," I said in a joking manner, so he wouldn't get offended. It was hiding, and the wine was still talking.

He moved my hands away, and I told him not to be ashamed.

Then I told him, "You remind me of a butterball stuffed turkey.

"What?"

"From now on, can I call you Butterball?"

He said, "Just not in front of his people."

I told him half of his people didn't give a damn about him anyway. They were just hanging around him to fit in or get in. He said he knew that, which was the reason why he is careful about who he had around him.

I saw a lot of things in him I didn't like. He felt like he had to put on this show around his people just so they could like him. You see how the overweight boy in school tries to be the funny one to get people to like him. That was Jazze Pha.

So I rubbed him down his thigh and massaged his dome. As I was massaging him, I was barely touching him, but he made sounds like it was painful for him. I asked him what was the matter, and he told me he was sensitive there. I didn't like the fact that he didn't smell fresh at all there, so I got up from the bed and asked him not to move.

I went into the bathroom, which was only a few feet away, got a wet soapy towel, and came in and washed his dome down while he relaxed there in bed.

Jazze grinned at me as if I was crazy or something. He didn't say a word, but stared at me as I washed him up. I asked him to not get offended, saying, I just like the fresh smell.

I didn't mean to offend him, but I had to tell him that I was really funny about hygiene. After I wet him all up, I gave him a hand towel and told him to dry off with it.

I think that spoiled everything, because I just couldn't bring myself to want this guy. Normally when I have had one too many drinks, it's on. Well, not that night. I told him I was way too messed up, that I needed to take a nap.

He told me that was fine because he had to be up at 5 a.m. to pick up his son from the nanny.

It was early in the morning, and he dropped me off first. I really liked him as a friend, and I knew he couldn't possibly have a woman to help him out with himself.

I think I felt sorry for him because I knew girls only wanted him for his money, and he should try to find someone to really like him for him, and not for his name.

So seeing it was 1 a.m. on the West Coast, where my girl Oobie was staying, I called her up and asked her if he was always so big, and she said no. He must have gained a lot of weight. Oobie knew of him because he was around when she worked with Little John and Too Short.

She is actually my sister (good friend) and she has sung on Fat Joe's album, and a lot of Lil Jon's hooks; as well as some work with Jeezy. Oobie also told me Jazze had changed because he was humble before.

After knowing him for a minute, he started to get real cocky with me, I guess, to show me he's the man. He had an opportunity to show me that night I had to wash him down, but it wasn't happening.

I would call him up and ask him what he was doing, and he would tell me he was hanging out with the fellas.

I would say, I'm coming down to the studio, and he would say, "Well, what time?" because he wasn't going to wait on me.

Then he would call me while he was out of town for no reason at all just to tell me which celebrity he was hanging out with and where they were. That didn't impress me at all. Hell, once you hang around Tupac and screw around with Suge, nothing else can really impress you.

Hanging around Michael Jackson would have impressed me though.

It turned me off more than anything did. After a while, he would call me in the late hours of the night, and I would answer his calls when I felt like it.

Not to talk about him in any way, but for him to be the person he was, come on now. You can't treat a girl like me any kind of way when I can slap your ego. But my objective wasn't to do that with anyone.

Around the same time, I had known Jeezy because we were introduced in Robins, Georgia at one of his promo parties by Will, the program director there.

Jazze somehow knew I was hanging around Jeezy and working with Shawty Redd as my producer. He clowned Shawty Redd, saying, he was all right, but everything he does is the same. So one night, Ciara was in the studio, and I brought my friend to the studio with me.

Jazze came from the engineering room and started acting funky with me. I pulled him in the break room and asked him what his problem was, and he said nothing. He told me that he didn't know I knew his boy.

I asked, "Who is your boy?

He said, "Jeezy."

I said, "Yeah, I did a song with him. We both work with the same producer, so hello, what's the big deal?"

There was no big deal. He was just being nosy and wanted to know my business. I didn't have sex with him, and he felt like Jeezy was just an artist, but he was the hot producer. So he told me to stick around that night, but my friend and I went out.

16

MIXING JEEZY WITH PLEASURE

Young Jeezy and I had started hanging out together. But at the time, we both were working with the same producer, Shawty Redd, who had seven songs on my album. I did a song with Young Jeezy called "Burning Up," and we were cool like that.

Jazze called me and asked me if I was going with

his boy. He just told me that wasn't cool, and if I was, it was no big deal, but let him know.

I said, "Look, Butterball, you got your life, and I got mine. You are not my man, and I am not your girl."

I have a problem with guys questioning me. I knew what that was all about. He thought Jeezy was hitting it, but at the time, he wasn't.

Young Jeezy and I did start hanging out more from working together with Shawty Redd and me doing hooks on his songs. We would hang out, and I would go to his promo shows.

I remember one night he asked me to go down to Albany, Georgia with him because he didn't want to ride down there with a bunch of guys. I told him I had just been down there doing a female show with Rasheeda and a few others on the marquee. Plus, it was too late notice. I had already made other plans to fly out to Miami the next day.

So I called Jeezy a few days later, and he asked

me if I wanted to go out to eat, and I said yes. He asked me to meet him at his place in Buckhead. At the time, he was staying across the street from Phipps Plaza.

I asked him how the show was, and he told me his show would have been better if I was there. He really wanted me to ride down there with him to Albany, Georgia. Really, Jeezy? Really? Okay! Men must think all females are stupid, with the things they say to us.

We ended up meeting up at Spondivits, a seafood place in Atlanta, and as I was walking in, I put it all together. I knew Young Jeezy had me come over to probably prove a point, because Jazze Pha and another guy were sitting at the table. Butterball acted like he didn't even know me like that, so I played along with him, knowing it wasn't that long ago I had to clean him up like a baby.

We sat at the same table. Jazze looked at me real funny, and when I spoke to him, he didn't speak

189

back. The whole time we sat there, he acted like a girl.

So Jazze picked up his phone, and I could clearly hear him talking to a female. He invited her down to eat with us, and when she arrived, she sat at the table next to him. Jazze couldn't keep his hands off the girl, hugging all up on her, like that meant something to me. I guess he was doing it to get my attention. But I didn't even like him like that.

Afterward, we all went to Magic City strip club and had a few drinks. I rode with Jeezy, and Jazze got in his candy red Cadillac convertible by himself. He had an attitude the whole time we were out together. I guess he thought Jeezy and I were involved, but we were not at the time. We were just friends.

After Jeezy found out Jazze had a little attitude with him, he rubbed it in a little more and told me that Jazze always acts like that with girls when he talked to them, as if they should like him over anybody else. He acts like he should be the one the girls are all over.

I didn't care. I was only there to have a good

time.

Jazze started complaining about the night, how the females were all tired, and he was tired of the strip club, which wasn't his thing.

So girls were coming up to Jeezy saying they liked his songs, and Jazze was sitting there being loud and drinking. He couldn't stand that Jeezy was getting all the attention. Then the girls asked me if I was Jara, the girl who sang "White Tee Girl Version," and I said, "Yeah, it's me."

Just as they were telling me how they loved the song, Jazze got up from his chair and said he was out of there for tonight, that he was bored.

How in the hell would any man be bored with all of those big-booty girls and naked everything in your face?

Eventually we all left the club for the night. Jazze got in his car, didn't say bye, and when he drove out of the parking lot, he was an inch away from running over my pretty feet.

So Jeezy and I got into his car on the way back to his spot. Then while we were in the car, my phone rang. Jazze called to ask me if I was with Jeezy, and if I was going home with him because that was his boy.

I asked him why. He said it was no big deal and that he should never even have asked me that. Then he hung up the phone. Jazze was tripping hard!

Jeezy was hitting the highway at 110 miles per hour. We got back to his place in less than 5 minutes. It was dangerous but fun, because the streets were empty late at night.

Jeezy asked me to come up upstairs, and I did. We talked for an hour outside on the balcony.

After we talked, we sat in the front room on the couch. The first thing he did was kiss me.

Hell, I was horny, so I went for it, thinking this guy could probably make me feel good. I couldn't wait to get it in with him. I wanted to see what he was working with, but I couldn't get a good feel through his jeans.

He took my skirt off and started licking me down below, which was okay. Then when he took his clothes off, he reached in his table drawer and got a condom out.

I couldn't get a good look at his dome because he slapped the condom on so quickly. And the next thing I know, we were having sex on his couch.

It felt okay, but I wanted to feel that intensity. I still couldn't get a good look, even when I turned over and let him hit it from the back. After a few strokes that way, it was over.

He asked me to stay the night with him. We went in the bedroom, where I fell asleep. I was so glad he wasn't a loud snorer.

The next morning, he asked me what I had planned for that day, and I told him I didn't know for sure. He asked me to call him because he wanted to go shopping. I told him I would call him as soon as I figured out my schedule.

But time didn't allow me to do that. As a matter of fact, I had a session to do later that day that I had forgotten about, so I called him up to tell him, and he said okay, that I should call him afterwards.

We never did have sex again, mainly because I didn't pursue it. There is only one shot with me, and it has to be really good in order for me to go ham on it and want more especially if it just sex with no benefits.. But we remained friends.

So I let it be known to him that he and I can't cross that line anymore, and he was all for it. Then he told me I would have to hook him up with one of my girls then, and I told him that's no problem.

I tried to get him with my girl who was head over heels for him. She probably would have had sex with him just because of who he was, whether the sex was good or not. Hell, most of the girls were crazy about Jeezy anyways.

Sometimes he would call me up from the studio

and sometimes ask me about meeting some of my friends. I told him most of my friends lived in L.A. When one of my friends did come to town, I told him she wanted to meet him, and his famous question was, Is she fine like you?

I brought one of my friends to the Ritz Carlton to meet him. So my girlfriend and I along with my other gay friend named Play all went and got something to eat there while we waited on him to get in from the studio.

He called, and we met him at the hotel. Jeezy wanted to have sex with my girlfriend because he liked girls with big booties, and she had a nice, big, round booty. So she told him it would cost him. He took his clothes off and laid down with the covers on top of him, butt naked.

Aisha didn't think he was attractive, but she was a fan of him. Aisha played with his penis while he was laying in the bed. I finally got a good look at it that night.

My friend Play called me on the phone from down in the lobby and asked me if he could come in and use the restroom. When he got to the door, I opened it up, and he went straight in to the restroom, with Jeezy still naked underneath the sheets.

Aisha kept playing around with Jeezy's dome and wrapped part of the sheet around it because he had a hard-on after she showed him her breasts.

With his dome sticking up from under the sheet, he asked her what she was going to do, because he was there to meet her when he should have been picking up his girl from the airport.

I said, "Dang, Jeezy! I didn't know you had a girl. What's her name?"

"Keyshia."

I still didn't know it was Keyshia Cole, until he said her last name. I looked at Aisha and said, "See how they do?" I started laughing. "Can't trust these men."

Jeezy told me to stop it because women do it too, and it's all part of the business.

I said, "True that!"

Then he said that he had one of his boys pick Keyshia up for him, but she was going to be upset with him because he was messing up, not answering her calls.

By that time, Play was done using the restroom. When he opened the door to the bathroom, you could smell the waste he had dumped in the toilet.

Jeezy asked me, "Why you bring this white boy in my room to stank it up?"

Play left out smiling because he saw Jeezy's dome with the sheet fitting around it, and of course, he was going to look.

So when my friend sat on the bed next to Jeezy, the two of them were going back and forth, because he wanted her to take her clothes off, and she wouldn't do it because she'd told him that he would have to pay her. He told her that he didn't pay for sex, but if she needed something, he would buy it for

197

her.

By then, I was messing with Jeezy and he told me that somebody need to get him off instead of playing with him. He said my girl got him all horny and then wanted to play with him, after he blew Keyshia off.

I got tired of the back and forth. If he knew he had to pick his girl up, he should have never met with us that night. It was clear Aisha wasn't going to have sex with him. Plus, Play was already waiting on us for well over an hour.

I thought Jeezy would be mad at me for what happened, but he said it was all good after I called him up the next day and apologized to him.

I had a problem with Jeezy's manager at the time, Coach. One day, I told him I didn't have VIP tickets to get in the club that night, and he told me that he got me. Well, when I went to the club, he didn't have it together for me, and he played me.

During all of that, Shawty Redd was still working on my album, so I had to concentrate more on what I was doing and avoid getting caught up in other people's lives.

17

SHAWTY REDD, "WHITE TEE" REMIX

I had recorded an answer to the "White Tee" song with my boy Shawty Redd. Dem Franchize Boyz had done the original version to the song "White Tee." Then there came remixes and different versions of the songs. The song was really popular on the mix tapes and the mix shows.

I met Shawty through a guy named C Dog, from the 404 Soldierz. Shawty ended up recording songs with me, and all were hot. At that time, I thought he was so little and cute. I would be flirting with him in the studio half of the time.

Out of the two months I hung out with him, I never had sex with him at that time. C Dog would always say Shawty wanted to know from him and the guy named Cass who I was chopping it up with. But I wasn't chopping it up with either of them. Sometimes I would bring Play with me to the studio, and he would tell me how Shawty would stare at me.

I told him I found Shawty to be real sexy and was wondering what his dome was like.

Shawty had just gotten his new red Benz, and Play and I asked him if he could take it out for a ride. He told him to take the keys and go. We all went to the store in the ride, with Play driving.

Shawty asked him to push the pedal to the floor, and

Play pushed it all the way to the floor on a small highway and flew right past the cops.

By that time, Shawty had separated from his stripper girlfriend, and I was glad. I didn't like the way she treated him anyway. So he asked me to come out with him for a minute, and I did. Play went in the house and waited for us, talking to another artist there.

Then Shawty asked me to ride with him. We went to a neighborhood somewhere, and he stopped in front of a house and asked me how I like it. The house was big and beautiful. It was dry wall and unfinished, but I know specs, and the house was impressive.

He told me it was a house he had just bought, that he was waiting on them to finish the construction on it.

Shawty looked at me and asked me what was to it. I told him I was single. So he asked me how long I was going to tease him, adding, he couldn't believe C Dog wasn't trying to hit on me. C Dog had nothing coming, in my eyes.

I knew of Shawty's girlfriend because she would come into the studio acting rude to him half of the time. I didn't want to screw her man and then look at her in the face. That wasn't happening. Had I never met her, and if I didn't have to be in the house with her, I would have been his JUMPOFF at the time, with pleasure.

He told me the relationship with her was over, that he wasn't going back to her. I told him I would have to see, because they were always back and forth with each other. He then said that she'd left him for one of his homeboys, that she'd been messing around with him for a while but he had recently found out about it.

He said he didn't know what it was, but I made him nervous. I didn't want him to have nervous feelings around me, I wanted him to feel comfortable. I had to tell him how sexy he was. As I was turning him on, he asked if he could kiss me. I then told him I wanted to see his dome, see what he was working with.

Shawty stood out of the car and showed me his dome. It had the right length to it, and it wasn't bad. It was actually pretty nice. It was curvy, but it was nice.

I let him feel on my breasts, and he said they were pretty, and big and perky. So, of course, we couldn't leave the night like that without me massaging his dome some. That night if he had a condom, I would have sexed him up, but neither of us had one.

Then he made a joke, asking me not to write about his dome in my songs, but his dome was exactly how I described it in my "White T" song.

While driving back to the studio, I told him, next time we record, I would like to screw him.

Out of everyone, I liked Shawty the most. I don't know why. I have to question myself, because he has the look of a thug. Though he was smaller than me, but he was sexy.

It wasn't long before he got into his new house. One day I went there, and we ended up in bed together.

He had the lights dimmed. That night, I was all over Shawty, and he knew how to handle all of what I had to give him.

He was better than anybody I had sex with in the business, besides my little actor friend, Clyde Jones. He put it down.

I was so hot that night, Shawty had to go a second round. I made him moan good, curling up his toes. It was special for me because I really found him attractive.

But I hadn't changed in other ways, because as soon as it was over, I got dressed.

Shawty wasn't ready for me to leave so soon. He said, "Damn, Jara! You just gon' hit a nigga and leave, huh."

But it wasn't like that with Shawty. I knew there

would be another time with us. Anytime, any day, I will have Shawty Redd whenever he says come on. The crush I have on him is huge, something about his swag. I lick my lips whenever I think about him. He isn't the best I have had, but I like him.

I left town the following week with my girl Ladee, Storm's friend, named Mariah, and her female friend named Renee. We all went to Miami for the weekend. We had a nice time, I saw Jeezy while I was there. I met up with some slip-and-slide folks I knew, and somehow we ended up at Diddy's house on Star Island that night. Beautiful home, black kitchen countertops, open view, just gorgeous.

I was tipsy that night, so I just remember riding. I do remember we all had to take our shoes off at the door because he had all-white carpet. I never saw Diddy at the time, because he was upstairs, and we didn't go upstairs that night. All I remember was, it was a hangout house, so me and the two girls were just hanging out, hoping Diddy would come down stairs and we could meet him..

Renee, Mariah's friend, was on the star-struck side. I heard her asking the guy who brought us to the house when was Diddy going to come out, and he kept saying he would introduce her to him, that he would be down shortly. So we went out back and sat on the lawn chairs and had some drinks.

Security told us it was fine to stay where we were because the two of them were smoking weed, and smoke was not allowed in Diddy's house. Security stood by the black glass door the whole time.

Now, mind you, we all had cell phones, but Renee picked up Diddy's house phone from the stand outside and made a phone call and was lounging on his house phone. I heard her talking.

All of a sudden I heard two security guys talking to Mariah. Then they walked up to Renee and told her she had to leave because that was Diddy's private line and his number could be all over the place. She'd insisted it was only one call she placed, but they didn't care.

They said we could stay, but she had to go. She got real funky with the guard and told him she didn't care about leaving anyway, and that Diddy wasn't nobody special. Mariah tried to keep her quiet because we only knew the guy who took us there, and he happened to be a close friend of Diddy.

So I told Mariah I didn't like causing problems like that, and that we should just leave because her friend was drunk. She was so bad, they were threatening to call the police on her. I don't remember much more about that night. I just know we were kicked out of Diddy's house, and it was daylight by the time we were dropped off the next morning.

On the ride back to Atlanta from Miami, I had a long time to think about my life and how I was moving forward.

Meanwhile, Mariah smoked her weed all the way back to Atlanta. But I wasn't cool with smelling like weed up and down the highway.

18

ONE-NIGHT STAND WITH GARY BUSEY

While I was visiting California again, a short while ago back in early 2000, my friend Lisa was invited to a party at a well-known producer's house in Beverly Hills, California. Lisa and I met through her boyfriend, who was an aspiring film director. One night she asked me if I wanted to go to a party with her and meet some film people, and I said sure.

When we arrived, I noticed I was the only brown sugar at this all-white party. At the back of the house, a live band was playing and there was plenty of food and drinks, so I got my party on, and mingled a little.

I was standing at the bar, on the outside patio of the house having a great time. Gary Busey flirted with me for a good hour before I decided to give him my attention. He saw the perfect opportunity to flirt more when Lisa stepped away from me.

I looked over at him and blew him a kiss. When I turned around, he'd stepped up to me. I smiled at him, giving him the "I-am-interested" signal. I asked him, was he Nick Nolte, because he looked like him. He thought it was cute of me to not know who he was, and introduced himself as Gary from Texas. I still didn't know who he was; I just thought he looked familiar.

He told me he was an actor, and that his friend, a film producer, owned the house we were at. Back then,

Gary was much more attractive and seemed genuine. We continued to talk for a while about acting and film stuff. He also told me he was producing a film with another producer.

He sat down next to me and stared me in the eyes. I don't know what happened, but the next thing I knew, my hands were on his penis. It felt real big. I had a thing for feeling guys penises. I was a little wasted that night, and he was too.

We got deep into the conversation, and the more we talked, the more my panties got wet. I asked him if he could show me where the bathroom was at, because the liquor was running through my body. So he took me inside of the house to the main master bedroom bathroom and came inside with me.

I thought it was sexy as hell. He watched me as I used the toilet and pulled out his penis to use it with me at the same time. I thought for sure he had some black in him somewhere, because I had experienced white guys before and had never run into one as big as Gary and he had a monster.

I asked him was it as good as it looks, and he told me to try it, and I did. He pulled my pants down, and we had sex on the bathroom floor. Gary was now the second man I have had sex with on the bathroom floor. Each time, the bathrooms were beautiful.

I stopped him after a few strokes, and he begged me to continue on. I used the excuse of not wanting Lisa to find out I was screwing him on the bathroom floor.

We went back downstairs, and we exchanged numbers. By that time Lisa was ready to go to Roxy, a nightclub on Sunset Boulevard. I was still a little wasted.

After we left the house party, I never did tell Lisa I had just screwed Gary on the bathroom floor. I didn't even know who he was really. I just knew he was attractive with a big penis and knew how to work it.

The next day Gary called me and invited me out to lunch over in Melrose, but I had already made plans to go out with another white man, the president of Worldspan at the time, who I'd met at Crustacean restaurant in Los Angeles while I was having dinner there with my girlfriend Lori. We briefly talked, but I was hardly interested when I became sober.

At the time, I really wasn't into white men. I was only enjoying the fabulous life he had to offer at the time. That's just the way it was.

A few days passed, and I hadn't answered Gary's calls. He stopped calling. He was my one-night stand. My JUMPOFF. Now, what did I get after that JUMPOFF experience? Absolutely nothing. But it taught me that some white guys are packing like the brothers.

I had never had a sexual encounter with the Worldspan president. Besides, I wasn't into old men at the time, and he was well into his senior years. I'm talking one foot in, and one foot out. But these days age doesn't matter to me at all. I especially love older men.

I must say, that yes I have experienced a lot of things in life. I have shared with you, only some of my experiences. Stay tuned, for JUMPOFF, volume 2.

ABOUT THE AUTHOR

At the tender age of eight, Jara began writing, acting and studying singing. In 1994, she joined a female singing group from Chicago on Columbia Records Label called "S.T.O.P." for one year. In 1995, she entered the Miss Illinois Pageant where she was crowned the Reining, *Chicago's Most Beautiful Girl.*

Jara continued to define and study her talent as a dancer, singer, rapper, actress which in turn, landed her a job, as a cast member, with Shelley Garrett Productions' "Beauty Shop 2." The show had a 23 state tour across the United States. Through this production, Jara was able to utilize her talents as a dancer and an actress.

While touring, Jara Everett decided she wanted to pursue acting in film and as a result was able to be casted in various acting roles including "Ladies of Englewood", an independent film produced by Kim

King and David Lee as well as other independent films.

In 2005, Jara found herself in the rap game after meeting Shawty Redd and 404 Soldiers. As a result, Jara rapped on various albums including being featured with 404 Soldiers *"We Some Riderz"* 2005; *"White Tee's Female Remake"* 2006; *"Trick Trick"* feat. Nate the Great 2006; *"Get Off Me"* feat. Shawty Redd 2006; *"Then"* feat. Young Jeezy *"Burning Up"* 2006. In addition, Jara sang background for the treo group Trillville *"Do it Then"* 2007.

Thanks for reading JUMPOFF, Been There, Done that! There's more to come from Hip Hops Mistress; Jara Everett.

In memory of my friend

Michael Clarke Duncan

(1957-2012)

I love you, Big Mike

PRINTHOUSEBOOKS.COM

Read it, Enjoy it, Tell A Friend!

Atlanta,GA.